Antonia Clare   JJ Wilson

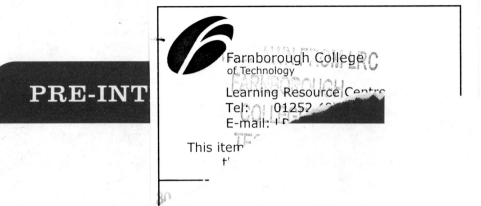

Farnborough College
of Technology
Learning Resource Centre
Tel: 01252
E-mail:

This item

PRE-INT

Total English

Workbook (with key)

Longman

Contents

Vocabulary | everyday actions

1 **a** Match a verb from A with a word or phrase in B.

A	B
1 read	a a bus
2 listen	b to bed late
3 get up	c on the phone
4 stay	d early
5 go	e your emails
6 chat	f nothing
7 watch	g in bed late
8 check	h to the radio
9 do	i TV
10 catch	j magazines

b Use the phrases above to complete the sentences.

You can *read magazines* while you are waiting for the dentist.

1 I always _____ when I get up in the morning.

2 I _____ with my sister every day.

3 I always _____ in my car.

4 I usually _____ to go to work.

5 On Saturdays I don't work, so I _____.

6 On Tuesdays I stay at home and _____ all day.

Grammar | likes and dislikes

2 **a** Complete the texts with words from the boxes.

> love   like   ~~stand~~   keen   hate

Andreas (26)
Germany

'I can't <u>stand</u> doing nothing. I really (1)_____ holidays where people lie on the beach all day – I can't understand it. I absolutely (2)_____ doing exercise so I get up early every day and run for ten kilometres before breakfast. I'm not very (3)_____ on team sports like football. When I go on holiday, I do water-sports like surfing and sailing. I quite (4)_____ walking and cycling too!

> mind   quite   love   stand   like

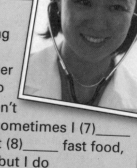

Seung Ah (24)
South Korea

'I absolutely (5)_____ eating good food. Cooking is very important in my culture. Usually my mother and my grandmother do all the cooking. They don't (6)_____ doing this but sometimes I (7)_____ helping them too. I can't (8)_____ fast food, especially hamburgers, but I do (9)_____ like Italian food, like pizza!

b **1.1** Listen and check your answers.

3 Complete the dialogues using phrases from the box.

> don't mind   quite keen on   not very keen on   really like
> ~~absolutely love~~   can't stand   like

  A: Do you like swimming?
  B: Yes, I *absolutely love* (+++) it. I swim in the sea every day.

1 **A:** Are you keen on tennis?
  B: I don't play, but I quite _____ (+) watching Wimbledon.

2 **A:** Do you enjoy watching football on TV?
  B: I _____ (+/-) it but it's better to go to the match.

3 **A:** Do you like walking?
  B: No, I don't. But I'm _____ (+) cycling.

4 **A:** Do you like watching boxing?
  B: No, I _____ (---) seeing people hit each other.

5 **A:** Do you watch a lot of TV?
  B: Not really, but I _____ (++) watching films sometimes.

6 **A:** Do you read novels?
  B: Yes, but I'm _____ (-) science fiction.

Reading

4 **a** Read the text quickly and match the headings in the box to the correct time of day.

> Stretch   Visit the dentist   Eat your dinner
> Think about a problem

b Read the text again. Mark the sentences true (T) or false (F).

1 Your brain works best in the middle of the day.
2 The best time to do a crossword is early morning.
3 It's a good idea to go to the dentist between 1 and 3 p.m.
4 Food tastes good in the early evening. This makes you hungry.
5 The best time to eat dinner is just before you go to bed.
6 It is good to do exercise in the evening because your muscles are warm.

A time for everything ...

What is the right time of day for your body to do everything?

Noon _____
Your brain works best at around midday. It's a good time to talk to your boss about a problem or do a difficult crossword.

2 p.m. _____
Do you hate going to the dentist? Make an appointment in the early afternoon. You don't feel pain so badly at this time of day.

5 p.m. _____
Are you very hungry when you finish work? This is because food tastes better in the early evening. Eating late is a bad idea. After midnight it is more difficult for our bodies to process fat, and this can give you heart problems.

8 p.m. _____
The best time to do exercise is around 8 p.m. At this time our body temperature is at its maximum, so our muscles are warmer.

Vocabulary | time phrases

5 Complete the sentences with the correct prepositions.

Mina

She gets up _at_ 11 o'clock every day.

1 _____ the afternoon she watches TV.

2 _____ about 8 p.m. she has a pizza at home.

3 _____ Saturdays she stays at home chatting on the phone.

Dan

4 _____ the summer, he goes to the beach to meet people.

5 He always goes out with friends _____ the evenings.

6 _____ weekends, he goes to parties or out to the cinema.

Sofia

7 _____ the mornings she reads the newspaper.

8 _____ Mondays she always goes to a museum.

9 _____ lunchtime she likes going to art galleries.

Listening

1 **a** 🔊 **1.2** Cover the tapescript. Listen and make notes in the table.

	Sleep weekdays (hours)	Sleep weekend (hours)	Insomnia (yes/no)	Alarm clock (yes/no)
Liz				
Paul				

b Answer the questions.

1 Who is always tired?

_____.

2 Who likes to stay in bed late on Sundays?

_____.

3 Who has problems sleeping when they are worried?

_____.

4 What happens to Liz when she drinks a lot of coffee?

_____.

5 Why does Liz use two alarm clocks?

_____.

6 When does Paul use an alarm clock?

_____.

TAPESCRIPT

Interviewer: So, how many hours do you sleep, Liz?

Liz: Not enough. I usually sleep about six hours on weekdays. That's why I'm always tired.

Interviewer: And you, Paul?

Paul: I get seven or eight hours sleep on weekdays. It depends what time I go to bed.

Interviewer: What about weekends?

Liz: Oh, I get more sleep at weekends – about ten hours. Sometimes I don't get up until lunchtime!

Paul: Really? I can't stay in bed that long. I usually sleep a bit less at weekends, about an hour less. Sometimes I try to stay in bed but then I just get up and start doing things in the house.

Interviewer: Did you know that ten per cent of the population suffer from insomnia – when you can't fall asleep. Do you ever get that?

Paul: Yeah, sometimes. When I'm worried about work.

Interviewer: And you, Liz?

Liz: No. I don't usually have any problems falling asleep. Very occasionally, I can't sleep if I've drunk too much coffee.

Paul: Yes, drinking coffee is a bad idea.

Interviewer: And do you use an alarm clock to wake up in the morning?

Liz: Absolutely. Yes. I can't wake up without an alarm clock. In fact, I have two because I turn the first alarm clock off, and fall asleep again.

Paul: I don't need an alarm clock usually. Sometimes I use one if I have to get up very early, to catch an aeroplane or something.

Vocabulary | daily routines

2 Complete the sentences below with one word. Write that word in the puzzle and find the hidden word.

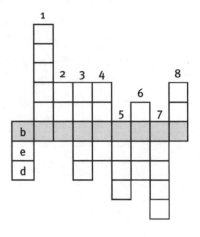

A: What time do you usually go to _bed_?

B: At about 10.30 pm. I usually read a book until 11 pm.

1 Do you have a _____ in the morning or the evening?

2 On Sundays I have a _____-in until about 11 am.

3 I like having a _____ in the afternoon, for example some fruit or chocolate.

4 I always _____ up very early in the morning.

5 I find it difficult to _____ asleep if I am worried about something.

6 When I am very tired I _____ a nap on the sofa.

7 Some nights I only _____ for about four hours.

8 I have to _____ up at 7 o'clock on weekdays.

Grammar | Present Simple

3 Complete the sentences using the verbs in brackets.

Sylvie _studies_ (study) French at university. She (1)_____ (not know) what she wants to do when she (2)_____ (finish) her degree. Sylvie (3)_____ (live) at home with her family.

Max (4)_____ (work) in the city. He (5)_____ (have) a new sports car, and a big house. He (6)_____ (enjoy) going out and spending lots of money. He (7)_____ (not smoke) and he (8)_____ (do) a lot of exercise in the gym.

Albert (9)_____ (not work) now. He's 75 years old. He usually (10)_____ (spend) his time at home. He (11)_____ (watch) TV and (12)_____ (read) the newspaper. Sometimes he (13)_____ (go) for a walk or (14)_____ (do) some shopping. He (15)_____ (not cook), so his daughter (16)_____ (bring) him food to eat.

4 Change the sentences to questions and write short answers.

You live in Monaco. (✓)

A: _Do you live in Monaco?_ B: _Yes, I do._

1 You like swimming. (✓)
   A: _____?
   B: _____.
2 They go to bed early every night. (✗)
   A: _____?
   B: _____.
3 She speaks Spanish. (✓)
   A: _____?
   B: _____.
4 He goes to university. (✗)
   A: _____?
   B: _____.
5 You have lots of homework. (✗)
   A: _____?
   B: _____.
6 We have her telephone number. (✗)
   A: _____?
   B: _____.
7 They remember you. (✓)
   A: _____?
   B: _____.
8 You want to come out later. (✓)
   A: _____?
   B: _____.

Grammar | adverbs of frequency

5 Rewrite the sentences using adverbs of frequency from the box.

> usually   hardly ever   sometimes   always   never   often

I go out with my friends in the evening. (40%)
I sometimes go out with my friends.

1 I forget to take my books to college. (5%)
   _____.
2 Jake is late. (0%)
   _____.
3 We see Pablo and Juan after the game. (60%)
   _____.
4 Do you drink coffee in the mornings? (100%)
   _____.
5 We visit my grandmother in France. (40%)
   _____.
6 It is sunny in August. (90%)
   _____.

Pronunciation | do/does

6 **a** **1.3** Cover the tapescript and listen. Write the questions and the answers you hear.

1 A: _____?
   B: _____.
2 A: _____?
   B: _____.
3 A: _____?
   B: _____.
4 A: _____?
   B: _____.
5 A: _____?
   B: _____.
6 A: _____?
   B: _____.

b Underline the stressed form of do/does/don't or doesn't. Practise saying the questions and the answers.

TAPESCRIPT
1 What do you do? I'm an artist.
2 Do you like going to the cinema? Yes, I do.
3 Do you have the tickets? No, I don't.
4 Does she know we're coming? Yes, she does.
5 Do you remember your dreams? No, I don't.
6 Does he have a car? No, he doesn't.

Grammar | Present Simple vs Present Continuous

1 Answer the questions about each picture. Write sentences.

I'm a teacher

Does he teach? *Yes, he does.*
Is he teaching now? *No, he isn't.*
What is he doing? *He's painting his house.*

I'm a bank manager

1 Does he manage a bank? _____.
Is he working now? _____.
What is he doing? _____.

We are musicians

2 Do they play guitar? _____.
Are they playing guitar now? _____.
What are they doing? _____.

I'm a French Student

3 Does she study French? _____.
Is she studying French now? _____.
What is she doing? _____.

2 Read the texts. Choose the correct alternatives.

My name is Becky, and I ('m) 'm being a dancer. I (1) *practise/am practising* for five hours every day, and I (2) *teach/am teaching* dance to a small group of children twice a week. At the moment, I (3) *dance/am dancing* with the National Dance Co. We (4) *perform/are performing* on Fridays in Covent Garden for the next two months. It is a great show, and I (5) *think/am thinking* I am lucky to be in it.

I'm Marc, and I am the manager of a bank in Hamburg. I (6) *work/am working* very hard, so I (7) *don't have/ 'm not having* much time to see my family. We (8) *like/are liking* going on holiday whenever we can. At the moment we (9) *ski/are skiing*. We (10) *stay/are staying* in a small resort near Mont Blanc for three weeks. The weather (11) *is/is being* wonderful and I (12) *learn/ 'm learning* some French too.

3 Complete the sentences using the Present Simple or the Present Continuous.

At the moment I *'m learning* (learn) to drive.

1 I _____ (not like) travelling by train.
2 Sue and Derek _____ (celebrate) their anniversary today.
3 Marta _____ (finish) school at 2 o'clock on Tuesdays.
4 Turn the TV off. I _____ (not watch) it.
5 Matt can't come to the phone at the moment. He _____ (have) a shower.
6 Sandra _____ (not work) today. She's doing her computer course.
7 Marc _____ (not think) it's a good idea to go to Spain.
8 My brother isn't working at the moment. He _____ (look) for a new job.

Reading

4 **a** Read the text and choose the best title.

- The future of shopping
- The coffee shop
- 24-hour banking for the future

It sells bread, milk and cigarettes. But *Shop 24* is not a good place to talk to the shopkeeper - because there isn't one.

Shop 24 is a new idea for shopping in the UK. It's a very big vending machine, the size of a shop. It's open twenty-four hours a day, seven days a week. Is this the future of shopping? We tried it. Our shopping list: eggs, milk, brown bread, ham, toilet roll, fresh coffee, aspirin, vegetables, chocolate. It starts well. *Shop 24* has eggs and milk. There are toilet rolls, aspirin, and lots of chocolate. But there is only white bread and there isn't any ham. There are no fresh vegetables and there is no fresh coffee.

I press the buttons to make our order. A big mechanical hand moves across the window. It picks up a box of eggs and drops it onto a shelf. The arm moves left and right collecting our order. It's fun to watch, better than normal shopping.

Then, disaster: the eggs are broken and the door closes before I can take my shopping out. Sandy is watching. He started *Shop 24*. He read about a shop like this in Belgium. Now there are two *Shop 24s* in town, and he hopes to introduce fifty more in the UK.

We finish our shopping in a local shop. It's much better than *Shop 24* but it isn't open twenty-four hours a day. We ask the cashier about the new vending machine shop. 'I think people will use it late at night. But people don't really like technology. Most people would prefer to talk to a face.'

b Read the text again and answer the questions.

1 What is different about *Shop 24*?

   a It has no staff.

   b It has no customers.

   c It sells robots.

2 What things from the list does the writer not buy from *Shop 24*?

   a brown bread, vegetables, aspirin, fresh coffee

   b brown bread, ham, vegetables, fresh coffee

   c white bread, ham, tomatoes, coffee

3 What problems does the writer have?

   a the eggs are old, and the door closes

   b the eggs are broken and there is no milk

   c the eggs are broken and she can't take her shopping out of the machine

4 The owner of the shop.

   a is from Belgium.

   b read about a Belgian shop like this.

   c went to Belgium on holiday.

5 They finish their shopping in

   a *Shop 24*.

   b a big supermarket.

   c another shop near *Shop 24*.

6 The cashier thinks that people will continue going to local shops because

   a customers prefer people to new technology.

   b *Shop 24* doesn't have enough things to sell.

   c local shops will stay open for twenty-four hours.

Writing

5 Find five more mistakes with double consonants.

From: Jo

To: Gloria

1 Hello Gloria,
   How are things in Spain? I hope you are
   well. Here everything is changing. Paul
   and I got maried, and we are starting a
5 new businness too. It's very exciting!
   We are opening a restaurant in the city
   centre called *JoJo's,* and we are going to
   serve Malaysian food.
   Everyone loves the food, but there are no
10 restaurants here at the moment. We are
   opening next month, so we are realy busy
   looking for staff, and making the restaurant
   look nice. I hope we finnish in time!
   I would love to hear what you are doing.
15 Are you still traveling a lot? When are you
   planing to visit us again? Hope to hear
   from you soon.
   Take care,
   Jo

Vocabulary | music

1 a Put the letters in the correct order and match them to the pictures.

1 adel isnreg _____ = picture _____
2 ocmreosp _____ = picture _____
3 dnab _____ = picture _____
4 rugiat _____ = picture _____
5 ceronct _____ = picture _____
6 lionocampit dc _____ = picture _____

b Match the sentence halves.

1 I'm really into Latin   a but I can't sing.
2 I downloaded   b last concert. It was
3 I love the   great.
4 I went to U2's   c music at the moment.
5 My favourite record is d lead singer. He's great.
6 I can read music   e their new song from
                            the Internet.
                        f a Bob Marley album.

Grammar | Past Simple

2 Read the texts. Choose the correct verbs from the boxes and put them in the Past Simple.

use   be   sing   win

> **ABBA**
> Swedish singer Agnetha Faltskog first (1)_____ in public when she (2)_____ five years old. Many years later, in 1974, her group, Abba, (3)_____ the Eurovision song contest and became world famous. In the 1990s the London musical *Mamma Mia* (4)_____ their songs. They are still one of the world's most popular bands.

meet   study   die   change   be

> **QUEEN**
> As a student, guitar player Brian May (5)_____ astronomy. When he (6)_____ Freddie Mercury, they started one of the world's most famous bands, Queen. Freddie Mercury (7)_____ born in Zanzibar and his real name was Freddie Bulsara. He (8_____ his name to Mercury when he became a singer. When Mercury (9)_____ of AIDS in 1991, there was a concert to celebrate his life. It was shown on TV in 76 countries.

perform   become   sell   start

U2

Four Dublin schoolboys (10)_____ this band in 1980 and had a hit with their first album, *Boy*. They (11)_____ even more famous after they (12)_____ at the Live Aid Concert in 1985. Their album *The Joshua Tree* (13)_____ over 10 million copies in the US alone. Always interested in politics, they also work to help the world's poor.

3 Write the questions for the answers, using the prompts.

A: (go/last night?) *Where did you go last night?*

B: I went to a concert.

1 A: (eat/for lunch?) _____?

B: We ate spaghetti.

2 A: (be/this morning?) _____?

B: I was in bed.

3 A: (do/Saturday night?) _____?

B: I played the guitar with some friends.

4 A: (leave/school?) _____?

B: I left when I was 18 years old.

5 A: (start/this job?) _____?

B: I started last week.

6 A: (instrument/play at school?) _____?

B: I played the piano.

7 A: (live/as a child?) _____?

B: I lived in London until I was 12.

8 A: (study/college?) _____?

B: I studied electronics.

4 Complete the sentences using the Past Simple affirmative or negative.

1 The book was boring. I _____ it. (like)

2 I _____ a party to celebrate my birthday. It was great. (have)

3 I _____ well because there was a lot of noise. (sleep)

4 She _____ a lot because she was very hungry. (eat)

5 The concert was too expensive, so they _____. (go)

6 We went to the best restaurant in London. The food _____ delicious. (be)

7 There was a film on TV last night, but we _____ it. (see)

8 She loves Colombia. She _____ there for six months. (live)

9 I was really busy yesterday so I _____ my homework. (do)

10 I _____ my sister a dress for her birthday. (give)

Pronunciation

5 **a** The verbs end with /t/, /d/ or /ɪd/. <u>Underline</u> the odd one out.

1 a kissed   b watched
  c played   d stopped

2 a wanted   b needed
  c waited   d washed

3 a lived   b worked
  c moved   d rained

4 a liked   b finished
  c ended   d wished

5 a believed   b loved
  c saved   d hated

b `2.1` Listen and check your answers.

How to ...

6 **a** Complete the sentences with the correct words from the box.

after   at   ago   as   up   of   in

a Six weeks _____ I sold my business for $2 million.

b _____ the mid 1990s I graduated from university with a degree in music.

c _____ a teenager I played four musical instruments.

d _____ working for a year in my old university I started my own business making musical instruments.

e I grew _____ in Lagos.

f I left school in the summer _____ 1990.

g I first became interested in music _____ the age of six.

b Put the events in order to make Ibi's life story.

1 e   2 __   3 __   4 __

5 __   6 __   7 __

Vocabulary | word families

1 Complete the text with the correct form of the words in brackets.

MusicSpa
Spa la la la

Are stress and (1) _____ (tired) a problem for you? Why not use your (2) _____ (intelligent) and take a break at Music Spa?! It's the most (3) _____ (relaxing) spa in Europe!

Many of our customers are (4) _____ (tired) after working hard all year. They come to Music Spa for (5) _____ (relaxing). We offer massages and music therapy. If you prefer more (6) _____ (energetic) activities, we have a 40-metre swimming pool. Or you can use your (7) _____ (imaginative) and join our painting course.

Enjoy the (8) _____ (relaxing) atmosphere at Music Spa. You will leave here full of (9) _____ (energetic)!

Visit www.musicspaprague.com for prices, availability and booking.

Pronunciation

2 a What is the stress pattern of the words? Write one word in each column.

> energetic energy relaxing intelligent
> imagination imaginative tiring

1	Oo	
2	Ooo	
3	oOo	
4	ooOo	
5	oOoo	
6	oOooo	
7	oooOo	

b `2.2` Listen and check your answers.

c `2.3` Listen and repeat the sentences.

1 He's really energetic.
2 I have no energy.
3 It's very relaxing.
4 She's really intelligent.
5 They have no imagination.
6 What an imaginative idea!
7 Running is tiring.

Grammar | *So do I/Neither am I*

3 Match the statements to the responses.

1	I'm hungry.	a	So was I.
2	I don't like cats.	b	I can.
3	I went to the cinema last night.	c	Neither do I.
4	I love rock music.	d	I was.
5	I didn't do any work today.	e	Neither did I.
6	I can't swim.	f	So did I.
7	I'm not a tourist.	g	I can't.
8	I was born in Paris.	h	I don't.
9	I can play the piano.	i	Neither am I.
10	I wasn't here yesterday.	j	So am I.

4 Complete the dialogues. Where there is (✓), agree. Where there is (✗), disagree.

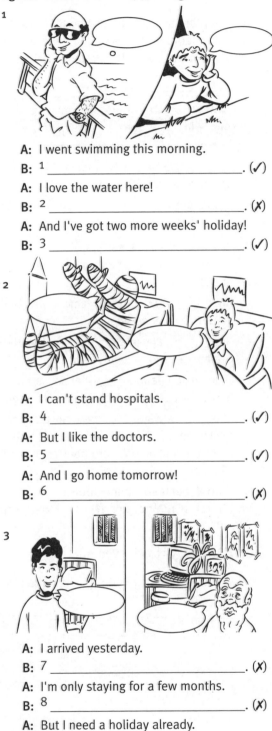

1

A: I went swimming this morning.

B: ¹ _____. (✓)

A: I love the water here!

B: ² _____. (✗)

A: And I've got two more weeks' holiday!

B: ³ _____. (✓)

2

A: I can't stand hospitals.

B: ⁴ _____. (✓)

A: But I like the doctors.

B: ⁵ _____. (✓)

A: And I go home tomorrow!

B: ⁶ _____. (✗)

3

A: I arrived yesterday.

B: ⁷ _____. (✗)

A: I'm only staying for a few months.

B: ⁸ _____. (✗)

A: But I need a holiday already.

B: ⁹ _____. (✓)

Listening

5 **a** ▸2.4 Two people talk about their favourite music. Cover the tapescript and listen. Complete the table with (✓) if they like this type of music, and (✗) if they don't.

	Jazz	Rock	Dance	Classical
Pavel	✓			
Helena				

b Read the tapescript. Complete the gaps with one word each.

TAPESCRIPT

Pavel

Well, I'm (1) _____ jazz at the moment. I bought this CD about three months ago and I really love it. I don't know anything about jazz, but I'm learning! In the past I (2) _____ to a lot of rock music, which I still like. I love (3) _____ like The Rolling Stones and Led Zeppelin. And I like dance music too. In fact the only (4) _____ I don't listen to is classical. I just find it boring. My parents always listen to classical music but I just don't like it.

Helena

I grew up listening to classical music. Mainly Beethoven, Mozart and a lot of Italian opera, and this is what I love listening (5) _____ in the evening. Also I'm (6) _____ into jazz music, especially singers like Louis Armstrong and Nina Simone. I (7) _____ love to sing like them or play an instrument, the piano or the guitar. I can (8) _____ music, but I can't play anything. So, yes, I love music but not all types. I don't like rock or dance music very much.

Lifelong learning

6 **a** Look at the notes this student made about a word.

> boring
> (1) **boring**   (2) (adjective)
> (3) not interesting
> (4) classical music is boring

b What information has the student written about the word? Write the number next to the type of information.

stress ☐1☐

example sentence ☐

definition ☐

part of speech ☐

Writing

7 Read the text. Find five mistakes and correct them.

I like many different types music. Hip hop is my favourite, but I also listen rap music. My favourite band is call Fugees. I love their CD, *The Score* – the songs are intelligent and have excellent tunes. Sometimes I am listening to classical music. I like Verdi and Puccini. I don't go in concerts because I prefer listening to music at home.

Grammar | Present Perfect

1 Choose the correct alternative.

A: Nick, tell us about your career.

B: (1) *I've made/I was made* 22 CDs and (2) *I've perform/I've performed* for the President many times.

A: Fantastic.

B: And (3) *I's won/I've won* 18 awards.

A: How many records (4) *you have sold/have you sold*?

B: (5) *I've sold/I'm sold* about 50 million.

A: (6) *Has you/Have you* ever wanted to do a different job?

B: No. I was born to be a rock star.

A: On your new CD, (7) *have you change/have you changed* your musical style at all?

B: No, I (8) *haven't changed/hadn't changed* anything. My fans love me as I am.

2 Complete the dialogues. Use verbs from the box in the Present Perfect negative.

> play   watch   taste   read   be   meet

1 **A:** Is this TV programme good?
   B: I don't know. I _____ it.
2 **A:** Do you like Rome?
   B: I don't know. I _____ there.
3 **A:** Is the spaghetti ready?
   B: I don't know. I _____ it.
4 **A:** Do you like the new computer game?
   B: I don't know. I _____ it.
5 **A:** Do you like Gabriel's new book?
   B: I don't know. I _____ it.
6 **A:** What do you think of Sam's new boyfriend?
   B: I don't know. I _____ him.

3 **a** Complete the sentences about Charlotte Church, Madonna and Whitney Houston. Use verbs from the box in the Present Perfect or Past Simple.

> change   watch   arrive   become
> sell   win   be   start

1 She _____ in New York, from Michigan, in 1978, with just 35 in her pocket.
2 Her albums _____ over 10 million copies before she was 18 years old.
3 She _____ her image many times.
4 She _____ her career as a model and a singer in 1981.
5 She _____ internationally famous with her first album *Voice of an Angel*.
6 She _____ many international awards. Her first Grammy was for *Saving All My Love For You*.
7 Nine million people _____ her concert at Brixton Academy in 2000, via the Internet.
8 She _____ always _____ very close to her family. Her brother Michael was her production manager, and another brother Gary has sung with her.

b Who is each sentence about: Church (C), Madonna (M) or Houston (H)?

Vocabulary | achievements

4 Read the text. Put the underlined verbs in the correct gap.

Musicians Exchange

Address: http://www.musiciansexchange.com

I was born in Denmark in 1980 and I started playing the violin when I was three years old. When I was 12, I (1) <u>wrote</u> a prize for Young Musician of the Year. I came to England to study music. I also (2) <u>won</u> English. I (3) <u>learned</u> my music exams in 1997 and (4) <u>started</u> to the United States to play with an orchestra. I (5) <u>made</u> articles for the *New York Musician* magazine and (6) <u>travelled</u> speeches at many music colleges. In 2004 I (7) <u>passed</u> my company MusiciansExchange. com. The company organises international travel for music students.

Reading

5 **a** Read the texts and answer the questions. Write NO (New Orleans), G (Glastonbury) or S (Salzburg).

1 Which festivals have different types of music?
2 Which festival doesn't keep the money it makes?
3 Which festivals happen outside?
4 Which festival is over 100 years old?
5 Which festivals have changed or grown bigger?
6 Which festival takes place in a city square?

b Look at the seven underlined words in the texts. What do they refer to?

The Salzburg Music Festival

The Salzburg Music Festival began, in a smaller form, in 1877. Since 1945, <u>it</u> has taken place every summer. For three weeks a year, Europe's best orchestras come and play the classics – Mozart, Beethoven, Strauss – at the festival. These days <u>its</u> programme also includes modern classical music. The beautiful seventeenth century square in front of Salzburg Cathedral is the perfect place for listening to the music of Europe's past and present.

New Orleans Jazz Festival

Jazz was born in New Orleans, and every year <u>the city</u> celebrates <u>its</u> birthday. The festival, which started in 1970, is full of colour, art, food and, of course, music. You can hear jazz, blues, rock, R&B, and gospel in the streets and concert halls of the city. Mahalia Jackson and Duke Ellington came to the first festival, and guest stars have included Lenny Kravitz, Van Morrison and LL Cool J. At the first festival there were only 350 people. Half of <u>them</u> were musicians. In 2001, 650,000 people came. *Life* magazine called it 'the country's very best music festival'.

Glastonbury

At the first Glastonbury festival in 1970 two thousand people came. Now, every year 150,000 people come. They dance in the rain, stay in tents and party for three days in the English countryside. All kinds of bands play <u>there</u>: U2, The Cure, Velvet Underground, and there is dance music, pop, reggae and classical music too. Glastonbury is fun, but it has a serious side. The organiser and owner of the land, Michael Eavis, says, '<u>It</u>'s not a charity event. It's a business which gives away all the money it makes.' The money goes to charities like Oxfam and Greenpeace.

c Change the underlined words. Use *it*, *they* or *its*.

1 The Summer Jam Festival takes place in Cologne. <u>The Summer Jam Festival</u> is held in July every year.
2 The festival started in 1986. <u>The festival's</u> original name was 'Loreley'.
3 In 1986 The Wailers came to the festival. <u>The Wailers</u> sang *No Woman No Cry*.
4 Many reggae bands attend. <u>The reggae bands</u> come from all over the world, including Africa and South America.
5 The festival attracts 25,000 people and is famous for <u>the festival's</u> atmosphere of peace and fun!

Vocabulary | food, drink, people, kitchen equipment

1 Match the things in the pictures to the words below.

1	knife = ___	7	cooker = ___
2	fork = ___	8	chef = ___
3	spoon = ___	9	customer = ___
4	ice cream = ___	10	spaghetti = ___
5	mineral water = ___	11	meat = ___
6	saucepan = ___	12	vegetables = ___

2 Complete the sentences using the words in brackets.

1 I'm not very keen on eating out. I prefer to stay at home and _____ _____ _____. (myself)

2 He eats hamburgers for breakfast, lunch and supper. The doctor told him to _____ _____ _____ fast food. (down)

3 He doesn't eat meat or fish. He's _____ _____. (a)

4 There is an excellent restaurant in Buckingham Street. It is owned by a _____ _____. (celebrity)

5 I am _____ _____ _____. I can only eat apples. (diet)

6 Sonia had a lovely _____ _____ last night. She cooked delicious food for everybody. (party)

7 Shall we _____ _____ tonight? Let's try the new Mongolian restaurant. (eat)

8 A: Would you like some chocolate?
   B: No, thanks. I _____ _____ chocolate last week. (up)

Listening

3 a **3.1** Cover the tapescript. Listen and choose the best summary.

1 Hannah likes eating out in restaurants with celebrity chefs.

2 Hannah is a vegetarian who likes eating at home.

3 Hannah doesn't cook so she eats a lot of fast food like pizza.

b Answer the questions. Listen and check your answers.

1 When did Hannah give up meat?

_____

2 Does she usually eat out?

_____

3 Does she like inviting people to eat at her house?

_____

4 Who cooks when she has dinner parties?

_____

5 Where does she get her new recipes?

_____

6 What is her favourite type of cooking?

_____

7 Is she eating a lot of pasta at the moment?

_____

8 Why/Why not?

_____

TAPESCRIPT

I'm a vegetarian. I gave up eating meat when I was at school because the food was so terrible. I like eating healthily so I usually stay at home and cook for myself. I don't usually eat out but there is a wonderful Indian restaurant near my house which does very good vegetarian food so I go there when I'm feeling lazy. I love cooking for friends so I have dinner parties quite often too. I like trying to cook new dishes. I watch the cookery programmes on television, where the celebrity chef has to cook a meal in just 20 minutes, and then I copy the recipes. I cook a lot of Italian food too. It's my favourite. I'm on a diet at the moment so I'm trying to cut down on pasta but it's not easy!

Vocabulary | phrases

4 Complete the text using the words from the box.

> success   chef   abroad   tasty
> experience   restaurant

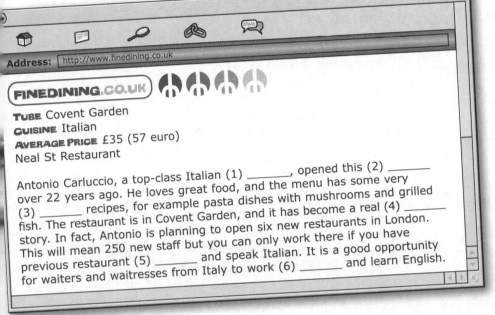

Address: http://www.finedining.co.uk

FINEDINING.CO.UK

TUBE Covent Garden
CUISINE Italian
AVERAGE PRICE £35 (57 euro)
Neal St Restaurant

Antonio Carluccio, a top-class Italian (1) _____, opened this (2) _____ over 22 years ago. He loves great food, and the menu has some very (3) _____ recipes, for example pasta dishes with mushrooms and grilled fish. The restaurant is in Covent Garden, and it has become a real (4) _____ story. In fact, Antonio is planning to open six new restaurants in London. This will mean 250 new staff but you can only work there if you have previous restaurant (5) _____ and speak Italian. It is a good opportunity for waiters and waitresses from Italy to work (6) _____ and learn English.

Grammar | *going to*

5 Look at the pictures and complete the sentences using *going to* and the verbs in brackets.

He isn't going to buy a new car. (buy)

1 She _____. (leave)

2 We _____ (win) the World Cup.

3 They _____. (play)

4 I _____. (be)

5 He _____. (pass)

6 They _____. (get married)

6 Complete the sentences using the correct form of *going to*.

1 Pete and Sal _____ (sell) their house.

2 Rob _____ (start) a new business in Australia.

3 _____ the builders _____ (finish) the work before May?

4 Jenny _____ (have) another baby in February.

5 We _____ (not have) time to see you before we leave.

6 _____ you _____ (visit) the pyramids when you go to Egypt?

7 We _____ (try) that new Turkish restaurant this evening.

8 I _____ (not be) at the party on Saturday.

How to ...

7 Find and correct the mistakes in these dialogues.

1 **A:** What are you going for your holidays?
   B: We're going visit my cousins in South Africa.

2 **A:** What your plans for next year?
   B: I going to look for a job because I need to earn some money.

3 **A:** What you going to do at the weekend?
   B: I'm going stay at home at Saturday to study.

4 **A:** What are you plans for when you leave university?
   B: I to go to work abroad.

Reading

1 **a** Read the texts. Which is positive and which is negative?

FAST FOOD IN A FAST WORLD

This film is set in Canada. The story is about Julie (Jane Wild), a waitress who has a date with a doctor named Carl (Tom Payne). She doesn't know that Carl already has an ex-wife and some kids. He doesn't know that she has an identical twin.

Fast Food in a Fast World doesn't have an exciting story or fast food. And it doesn't have any laughs. When Julie receives lots of money from a relative who dies, it is the happy ending to the story. But unfortunately, this is a poor quality movie.

My Big Fat Greek Wedding

This is the story of 30-year-old Toula, who falls in love with Ian (Corbett). The only problem is that he's not Greek. According to the film, Greek women should get married (to Greek men), have lots of babies and feed lots of people. Will her family be happy if she marries a non-Greek? Maybe not. Will they accept her decision when they see that she is happy? The answer is yes and the rest of the film is about the wedding.

It's not a great story but the film is very funny. The first hour, when we learn about the relationships in a Greek family, has some very good humour.

My Big Fat Greek Wedding shows us a traditional wedding and at the same time talks about accepting people who are different from us.

b Mark the sentences true (T) or false (F).

1 *Fast Food in a Fast World* is a film about women doctors.

2 The story ends happily when Julie gets some unexpected money.

3 *My Big Fat Greek Wedding* is about a young Greek couple who get married.

4 It is a funny film, which talks about Greek family relationships.

c Find words or phrases in the texts which mean:

1 go to a restaurant or film, etc. with someone you like in a romantic way _____

2 informal word for children _____

3 US word for film _____

4 to say yes to something/to agree _____

Pronunciation

2 **a** **3.2** Listen and underline two words in each sentence with silent letters.

1 My daughter hurt her knee.

2 The writer thought about her book.

3 It was a cold night in autumn.

4 There were eight foreigners.

5 Could you take the dog for a walk?

6 I know you're wrong.

7 The sign was high in the sky.

b Write the words in the table.

Silent *g*	Silent *w*	Silent *l*	Silent *k*	Silent *n*
daughter				

c Listen and repeat the sentences.

Grammar | relative clauses

3 **a** Complete the crossword clues with *who*, *which* or *where*.

Down

1 It's the person _____ serves your food.

2 It's something _____ is very cold and you can eat it at the end of a meal. (3,5)

3 It's someone _____ eats in a restaurant.

4 They are the instructions _____ you use for cooking a particular dish.

7 They are things _____ you use for cutting.

8 It's the meal _____ you eat in the middle of the day.

Across

5 It's the dish _____ you eat before your main course.

6 It's a place _____ you can buy fresh fruit and vegetables.

9 It's the room _____ a chef works.

10 It's the person _____ cooks your meal.

b Use the clues to complete the crossword.

4 Match the sentence halves. Make complete sentences with *who*, *which* or *where*.

1	A builder is someone	a	flies planes.
2	A cooker is a machine	b	writes books.
3	An airport is a place	c	tells you what food you can eat.
4	A pilot is someone		
5	A pencil is something	d	you use for writing or drawing.
6	An author is someone		
7	A cinema is a place	e	builds houses.
8	A menu is something	f	makes food hot.
		g	people catch planes.
		h	you can watch films.

Lifelong learning

5 Put the words in the correct order to make sentences.

1 use It's bottles. for opening which you something

2 yourself. that thing you It's to the dry use

3 stuff bread. can put It's you the on which

4 changing the for which thing the TV. you on use It's programme

5 can It's cook that you in. something

6 your the put It's food. that stuff you white on

Writing

6 There are twenty mistakes with spelling, punctuation or capital letters in this letter. Find the mistakes and correct them.

Dear Anna,

Thanks for your letter. Im sorry I didn't reply sooner, but I only recieved the letter this morning. I have been away on holiday whit my sister, and I only came home yesterday. We went camping in Cornwall, wich was beautifull exept for the wether. It rained nearly every day!

Its very kind of you to invite me to stay. I would love to come to scotland, and it would be great to see you again. We havn't seen each other for nearly tow years now – I can't belief it. I could come for the last weekend in september (27th / 28th). I am finishing my job, so I will have a few days free. Would that be OK with you?

Anyway, I hop youre well, and I am looking foward to hearing your news. How is your course going. Are you still planing to open a flower busness when you finnish?

Speak to you soon.

Love,
Paola

Vocabulary | adjectives to describe food

1 Three sentences have mistakes. Find the mistakes and correct them.

1 Did you make this chocolate cake? It's very delicious!

_____

2 I can't eat snails. I think they are absolutely disgusting!

_____

3 This fruit salad looks mouth-watering. Would you like some?

_____

4 I don't think the soup is very good. It's a bit tasty.

_____

5 That meat looks very horrible. I think it's old.

_____

6 This magazine is full of tasty recipes.

_____

2 Complete the text with words from the box.

> appearance dishes high quality location texture

Great Ideas for Restaurant Owners

The area

The most important thing is to find a good (1)_____ for your restaurant. Why get (2)_____ marks for your menu if there are no customers?

The chef

Find an experienced chef but make sure you try his cooking first. The food has to have a good (3)_____ and (4)_____ and has to taste delicious too!

Ask the chef to cook you a few different (5)_____ from the menu, so you can be sure he can cook the recipes you want.

The food

You need to know where to buy top (6)_____ food for your menu. Your chef may know so ask him/her first.

3 Choose a verb from A and an adjective from B to complete the sentences.

A	B
looks feels smells tastes sounds	delicious expensive old soft horrible

1 Not again! That music _____ _____.

2 I don't think it's any good. It _____ _____.

3 This jumper _____ so _____.

4 This meal _____ _____

5 That dress _____ _____.

Grammar | Present Continuous

4 Complete the sentences with the Present Continuous and the words in brackets. Use contracted forms where possible.

1 A: What _____ (you/do) this evening?
   B: I _____ (stay) at home and _____ (watch) television.

2 A: _____ (you/cook) supper later?
   B: No. We _____ (have) a takeaway pizza.

3 A: _____ (you/do) anything this afternoon?
   B: I don't know. I _____ (not play) tennis with Pete because _____ (rain).

4 A: How _____ (you/get) home from the meeting?
   B: I _____ (not drive). I _____ (catch) the six o'clock train.

5 A: _____ (you/come) to the football match on Saturday?
   B: Yes. We _____ (bring) a friend too.

6 A: We _____ (not go) on holiday next week.
   B: Why not?
   A: Matt _____ (go) to hospital.

7 A: Help! I'm not ready.
   B: Don't worry. The guests _____ (not arrive) until 8.30.

8 A: _____ (you/come) to the office on Monday?
   B: No. I _____ (not work) next week.

5 Complete the sentences with verbs from the box in the Present Continuous.

> meet move leave finish go
> catch work have play visit

1 We _____ sailing this weekend on Jack's new boat.
2 They _____ for France on Friday morning.
3 I _____ the Natural History Museum this afternoon.
4 He _____ the bank manager tomorrow morning.
5 _____ you _____ football on Saturday?
6 We _____ not _____ house this month.
7 She _____ a baby soon.
8 _____ they _____ a train to Venice?
9 We _____ on this project for two weeks.
10 He _____ the painting tomorrow.

How to ...

6 **a** **3.3** Listen to Jim inviting two women out. Write notes in the table.

Sal	Bella
Plans: *staying at home*	Plans (Sat):
Reason:	Reason:
	Plans (Sun):

b Write sentences to say what the women are doing at the weekend.

1 Sal *is staying at home to study for her exams.*
2 On Saturday, Bella ...
3 On Sunday, Bella ...

c Number the lines of the dialogues in the correct order. Listen again to check.

Dialogue 1

☐ Hello Jim.
☐ Thanks Jim. I'll tell you ...
☐ Not really. I'm staying at home to study for my exams.
[1] Hello, Sal. It's Jim.
☐ OK. I'll call you again next week. Good luck with your exams!
☐ Oh, that's really nice of you but I don't like going out when I have to study. I'm sorry. Perhaps another time?
☐ Are you doing anything this weekend?
☐ I see. Well, why don't you come out for a drink on Saturday evening? There's a new bar opening on the river ...

Dialogue 2

☐ What are you doing on Saturday evening?
☐ Hello, Bella? It's Jim.
☐ Perfect! I can meet you on the river at 7 p.m.
☐ Nothing. Why?
☐ 7.30 would be better for me. I'm going to Oxford on Sunday to visit my aunt and I'm driving so I won't be back ...
☐ Well, would you like to come out for a drink, or something to eat?
☐ Hello.
☐ Great idea! Oh, wait a minute. Saturday? No, I've just remembered. I'm going to a concert on Saturday. Diane's bought some tickets to see Guns and Roses. Why don't we go out on Sunday evening?

Present Simple vs Present Continuous

1 Underline the correct verb form.

1 *Are you leaving /Do you leave* now?
2 Sam *doesn't usually wear /isn't usually wearing* jeans.
3 I *am never watching /never watch* TV.
4 Who *does James talk /is James talking* to?
5 *Do you know /Are you knowing* my wife, Samira?
6 She *is sometimes going /sometimes goes* out.
7 A: Can I help you?
   B: I *look /am looking* for this dress, in size 12.
8 The manager *often has lunch /is often having lunch* in his office.
9 A: What *are you doing/do you do*?
   B: I'm waiting for the train.
10 It *doesn't rain/isn't raining* now.

2 Write the questions. Match them to the answers a–j.

1 What / you / do?

_____

2 Where / you / go?

_____

3 What / she / eat?

_____

4 Where / they / live?

_____

5 What time / you / get home?

_____

6 You / go / the shops?

_____

7 What / Paul / do?

_____

8 You / enjoy / your course?

_____

9 How / get / to work?

_____

10 Jayne / have / a car?

_____

a Yes. Do you want me to buy something?
b No, she doesn't.
c In South Africa.
d I walk.
e To the dentist. I've got an appointment.
f I'm a teacher.
g Usually at about 7 p.m.
h Yes. I'm learning a lot.
i He's playing tennis.
j Vegetable soup with pasta.

Past Simple vs Present Perfect

3 Choose the correct verb form.

Goddesses

The Goddesses are a new girl band from Dublin. They (1) *started | have started* playing in 2002, and (2) *have made | made* fourteen albums. Their first album (3) *sold | has sold* 50,000 copies in the first two months. They (4) *have won | won* the Irish Music Awards twice, and (5) *have toured | toured* around Europe and America. Why (6) *have they been | were they* so successful?

Amy and Sam, the lead singers, are sisters. 'We (7) *have always loved | always loved* singing. When we were at primary school we (8) *started/ have started* a band with some friends and (9) *sang | have sung* in a concert at the end of the year. It (10) *was | has been* a great success. Since that day we (11) *have always been | were always* very lucky.'

4 Complete the dialogues using the Past Simple or the Present Perfect.

1 A: _____ you ever _____ (go) to Brazil?
  B: Yes. I _____ (go) to Carnival in Rio last year.

2 A: I _____ (live) in Rome for five years now.
  B: Why _____ you _____ (move) there?

3 A: _____ you _____ (visit) any interesting sights in Beijing when you were there?
  B: No. We _____ (not have) enough time.

4 A: _____ you ever _____ (see) any famous bands in concert?
  B: I _____ (see) Pink Floyd when I was a teenager.

5 A: _____ you _____ (watch) the Spiderman film on television last night?
  B: No. I _____ (see) it three times already.

Going to and Present Continuous (for future plans/arrangements)

5 Correct the mistakes in the sentences.
1 We leaving on Friday at 2 p.m.
2 Are you go to see Tariq this weekend?
3 I'm have lunch with my mother tomorrow.
4 We is meeting in Hyde Park.
5 Do they coming to the party tonight?
6 I amn't flying to Hong Kong.
7 He is to go to buy a new computer later.
8 We aren't going drive through the mountains.
9 Is Mark to playing football on Saturday?
10 Maria isn't comes to the restaurant.

Defining relative clauses

6 Complete the sentences using *which, who* or *where*.
1 It's the place _____ I like to sit and read.
2 She is someone _____ I can talk to.
3 It's the thing _____ you use for cutting food.
4 That's the film _____ I told you about.
5 This is the office _____ we can work.
6 That is the theatre _____ I saw my first concert.
7 He is the man _____ told me about the job.
8 It is the grammar _____ I find difficult.
9 That is the restaurant _____ we met.
10 It's something _____ you use for opening a bottle.

7 Put the relative clauses (a-g) in the correct place in the sentences (1-7).
a who has his own software company
b which you can't find
c which has double rooms for 50 euros
d where we had our first meal together
e who offered me her seat on the bus
f ~~which you gave me~~

1 I can't find that bag.
   I can't find that bag which you gave me.
2 Are these the keys?
   _____
3 Do you remember the restaurant.
   _____
4 Do you know the name of that hotel?
   _____
5 That's the woman.
   _____
6 My sister introduced me to a man.
   _____

Vocabulary

8 Put the words and expressions in the box into the correct groups.
1 food
2 daily routine
3 shops
4 music
5 adjectives

classical   compilation CD   concert
customers   delicious   disgusting   energetic
fall asleep   get a takeaway pizza   get up
early   go clubbing   intelligent   lamb
lead singer   mineral water   onion   play the
violin   products   read a magazine   shop
assistant   staff   tasty   vegetable   yoghurt

9 Complete the sentences using the words from the box.

into   relaxed   distinction   tasty   cook
download   checked   picnic   nap   started

1 Do you _____ for yourself or do you prefer to eat out?
2 I'm very tired. I think I'll have a _____ this afternoon.
3 It's a very sunny day. Why don't we buy some food and have a _____ in the park?
4 I'm really _____ jazz at the moment.
5 I don't buy CDs anymore. I usually _____ music from the internet.
6 I had a hot bath and a massage, and I felt very _____.
7 Tim is working very hard because he has just _____ his own company.
8 This is a very _____ recipe. I've never cooked apples like this before.
9 I have been away so I haven't _____ my emails for a few days.
10 I passed my exam with a _____!

Vocabulary | collocations

1 Put the underlined letters in order to complete the sentences.

1 I held my btrahe when I was under the water.
2 I don't have the ahpcsiyl eshrtgtn to swim for two hours a day.
3 You need netlam strength to cope with bad news.
4 I tcdenrlloo my fear under water, but it was difficult.
5 We lyre on our colleagues because we can't work alone.
6 I haven't cahevide my goals. I want to travel the world.
7 The biggest ehlgclena in sport is winning an Olympic medal.

Grammar | comparatives

2 a Read the texts.

ABT EXTREME SPORTS HOLIDAYS

Kayaking, mountain climbing, base jumping and free diving.

ACCOMMODATION:
4-star hotel, all meals provided.

YOU NEED TO BE:
over 16, a strong swimmer, very fit.

COST:
$500 for one week or $1,500 for one month.

Knockout Vacations

Try 15 extreme sports! Minimum age is 18.
No experience necessary. Beginners welcome.
Non-stop fun and games!

Accommodation: simple flats for 6 people.
Price: $349 per person. All vacations last 7 days.
For a knockout holiday you will never forget!

b Complete the sentences using the words in brackets.

1 These courses at ABT are _____ _____ _____ (expensive) the courses at Knockout.
2 ABT has _____ (good) accommodation _____ Knockout.
3 Knockout sounds _____ _____ _____ (enjoyable) ABT.
4 Knockout seems _____ _____ (friendly) ABT.
5 You can do _____ (long) courses at ABT.
6 Knockout has a _____ (great) variety _____ ABT.
7 ABT welcomes people who are _____ _____ (young) 18.
8 For ABT you need to be _____ _____ (fit) normal people.

3 a Correct the sentences.

1 This one isn't as fast than the other one.
2 It was much more bad this morning. It rained for hours.
3 It was most interesting than his last one, and I liked the acting.
4 This one is more cheap than the other place, and breakfast is included.
5 She's crazyer than her sister.
6 It's gooder than my last one because I have more independence.

b What are the sentences in Ex. 3a about?

cars   people   hotels   weather   films   jobs

4 Do the pairs of sentences have the same or a different meaning? Write S for the same, D for different.

1 a Keisuke was younger than Joe.
  b Joe wasn't as old as Keisuke. ____
2 a The Hilton is more expensive than The Marriott.
  b The Marriott is cheaper than The Hilton. ___
3 a I can run faster than my brother.
  b My brother can't run as fast as me. ___
4 a The first exam wasn't as easy as the second.
  b The second exam was more difficult than the first. ___
5 a My French isn't as good as my German.
  b I speak better French than German. ___
6 a Today we walked further than yesterday.
  b We didn't walk as far yesterday as we did today. ___

5 Rewrite the sentences so that they mean the same. Use the adjectives in brackets. Change the form if necessary.

1 The Atlantic is 76.762 million square km. The Pacific is 155.557 million square km. (big)

The Pacific _____ the Atlantic.

2 Free diving is dangerous. Swimming isn't dangerous. (dangerous)

Free diving is _____ swimming.

3 Mountain climbing is difficult. Without oxygen it is very difficult. (difficult)

Mountain climbing with oxygen isn't _____ mountain climbing without oxygen.

4 Physical strength is important for divers. Mental strength is very important. (important)

Physical strength _____ as mental strength, for divers.

5 Temba Tsheri climbed Everest when he was 15. Sherman Bull May climbed Everest when he was 64. (old)

Temba Tsheri wasn't as _____ Sherman Bull May when he climbed Everest.

6 Junichi Koide dived 132 metres. Tanya Streeter dived 160 metres. (deep)

Tanya dived _____ Junichi.

Vocabulary | adjectives to describe people

6 Write the words in the correct places and find the hidden word.

1	g	e	n	o	r	o	u	s
2								
3								
4								
5								
6								
7								
			e					

1 She gives lots of presents to her friends. She's really _____.

2 No one can stop him when he wants something. He's really _____.

3 She solves problems and understands things easily. She's _____.

4 She is sure that she is good enough. She's very _____.

5 He wants to be manager of this company by the time he's 30. He's _____.

6 She wasn't frightened when she saw the lion. She's very _____.

7 He's good at basketball, he's a great artist and he speaks five languages. He's very _____.

Reading

7 Read the text. Mark the sentences true (T) or false (F).

1 Robert Garside has run across seven continents.

2 Garside robbed someone in China.

3 He split up with his girlfriend during his journey.

4 He went to prison in Australia.

5 He carries a photo of Nelson Mandela.

6 He listens to music.

7 He runs about 9,000 miles a year.

8 He thinks he is a normal person.

Running Man

His friends call him Running Man. Thirty-three-year-old Robert Garside has run through four continents – Australia, Asia, Europe and South America – on an incredible three-year journey. Now he wants to be the first person to run across all seven continents.

His journey has had problems. In Russia, someone tried to shoot him. In China, police put him in prison for five days. In Pakistan, he was robbed and left with just his clothes and passport. When he called his girlfriend to tell her, she ended their relationship! In Australia, police stopped Robert when they found him running in 55 degree heat.

Robert travels lightly. He carries a walkman with cassettes of Pavarotti and Beethoven, a letter from Nelson Mandela and a camera. He runs for eight hours each day, and he hopes that his journey, a total of 45,000 miles, will take five years. His friends think he is crazy. He says, I just wanted to do something different. I'm a very normal person.

Vocabulary | survival

1 Match the sentence halves.

1 I'm good at coping   a challenges in my job.
2 I learned survival   b with problems at work.
3 There are many big   c I love the wilderness.
4 I like to push   d a shelter at survival school.
5 I live in a city but   e skills in the army.
6 We learned to build   f myself to the limit.

2 Read the text. Complete the gaps with words from the box.

skills   challenges   myself   wilderness   cope   shelter

Hello,

My name is Billy Bones. I have lived on a desert island for about two years. Living here is full of big ¹_____. I learned survival ²_____ on this island and I built a ³_____ because it rains a lot. But I'm happy now. I can ⁴_____ with any problem and I love to push ⁵_____. So why am I writing this letter? Because the ⁶_____ is very messy and I'm looking for a cleaner. Please write back.

BB

Grammar | superlatives

3 Write sentences. Follow the examples.

I've eaten some good food, but this is the best.
I've seen some beautiful countries, but this is the most beautiful.

1 watch/boring films
_____

2 have/bad days
_____

3 play in/great games
_____

4 live in/quiet places
_____

5 stay in/expensive hotels
_____

6 have/long conversations
_____

7 learn/important lessons
_____

8 have/crazy moments
_____

4 Read the text and make superlatives from the words in brackets.

SURVIVOR!

It's Big Brother, but on an island! Who will survive this time? Here are the four remaining contestants.

Mike is physically (1)_____ (strong) contestant. He loves nature and he likes to push himself to the limit. He isn't (2)_____ (intelligent) contestant.

Clara is from Ancona, Italy. She loves water and she is (3)_____ (good) swimmer in the group. She is (4)_____ (small) contestant but she has many survival skills.

Yevgeny likes challenges. He was in the Russian army for five years. He says it was (5)_____ (hard) time of his life but he enjoyed it. Yevgeny is (6)_____ (popular) contestant because he has a good sense of humour.

Virginia is (7)_____ (tall) contestant. She played basketball for the US women's team. Now she works in a survival school. She is (8)_____ (fit) person in the group.

5 Write sentences with the same meaning. Use the words in brackets. Write 2–5 words.

1 No runner is faster than Lewis. (the)

Lewis _____ runner in the world.

2 I have never eaten better food! (ever)

This is the _____ eaten!

3 There were not many easier exams. (of)

This was one _____ exams.

4 No other country in Europe has more tourists than Italy. (popular)

Italy is _____ tourist destination in Europe.

5 I've never stayed in a house this beautiful. (have)

This is the _____ ever stayed in.

6 The other theatres in the town are bigger than this one. (theatre)

This is _____ the town.

7 He is 100 kg. The other boys are not so heavy. (is)

He _____ boy in the group.

8 None of the other songs on the CD are as good as this. (the)

This is _____ song on the CD.

Pronunciation

6 **a** Match the pictures to the phrases.

1 The biggest day of your life. ___

2 The best book of the year. ___

3 The tastiest snack of the day. ___

4 The funniest programme on TV. ___

5 The fastest machine on the road. ___

6 The hottest show in London. ___

b Each phrase has three stressed words. Mark the stress.

> **TAPESCRIPT**
>
> 1 The biggest day of your life.
> 2 The best book of the year.
> 3 The tastiest snack of the day.
> 4 The funniest programme on TV.
> 5 The fastest machine on the road.
> 6 The hottest show in London.

c **4.1** Listen and repeat.

Writing

7 Choose the correct words to complete the letter.

> Dear Josie,
>
> A (1)_____ thank-you for last Saturday. I (2)_____ a really good time and the barbecue was great (3)_____.
> The fish was the most delicious I've (4)_____ tasted!
> Also, thank you for (5)_____ me to cook shrimps! We (6)_____ love to do it again, but next time in our garden!
> (7)_____ wishes,
>
> Marcin

1	A	small	B	big	C	great	D	real
2	A	enjoyed	B	spent	C	had	D	was
3	A	funny	B	enjoyable	C	fun	D	time
4	A	ever	B	always	C	been	D	never
5	A	help	B	teaching	C	making	D	show
6	A	would	B	will	C	do	D	can
7	A	Love	B	Kind	C	Nice	D	Best

Grammar | indirect questions

1 Put the words in the correct order to complete the questions.

1 what is the time
Can you tell me _____?

2 can an Internet café find where I
Do you know _____?

3 the tube is nearest where station
Do you know _____?

4 what leaves the time next train
Can you tell me _____?

5 Sunday on is the if museum open
Do you know _____?

6 a costs ticket how much
Can you tell me _____?

7 to airport how is far it the
Do you know _____?

8 phonecard I where can buy a
Can you tell me _____?

2 a Change the questions to make them indirect.

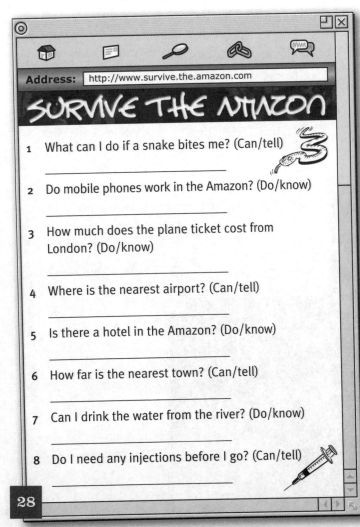

SURVIVE THE AMAZON

1 What can I do if a snake bites me? (Can/tell)
_____

2 Do mobile phones work in the Amazon? (Do/know)
_____

3 How much does the plane ticket cost from London? (Do/know)
_____

4 Where is the nearest airport? (Can/tell)
_____

5 Is there a hotel in the Amazon? (Do/know)
_____

6 How far is the nearest town? (Can/tell)
_____

7 Can I drink the water from the river? (Do/know)
_____

8 Do I need any injections before I go? (Can/tell)
_____

b Match the questions in Ex. 2a to the answers.

Address: http://www.survive.the.amazon.com

SURVIVE THE AMAZON

a It is at Belém. Question ___

b There are many cheap hotels in and around Belém. Question ___

c Prices vary, but usually between $700 and $1,000. Question ___

d You need an injection against yellow fever. Question ___

e Try to identify the type of snake. Tie a bandage around the bite and go to the doctor. Question ___

f Probably not far. There are many small towns along the river. Question ___

g Only for local calls. Question ___

h It is safer to boil the water first. Question ___

Listening

3 a [4.2] Listen to the dialogues. Where are the speakers? Choose a place from the map.

Dialogue 1 = *Camden Market*

Dialogue 2 = _____

Dialogue 3 = _____

Dialogue 4 = _____

Dialogue 5 = _____

Dialogue 6 = _____

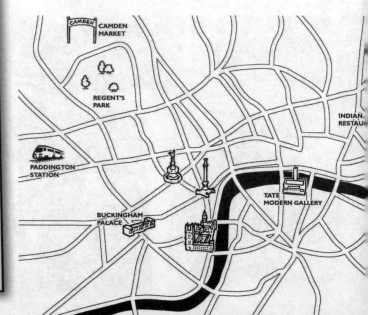

b Complete the dialogues. Write one word in each gap.

1 A: Can you tell me what time it (1) _____?
   B: What, the market?
   A: Yes.
   B: (2) _____ 6.00.
   A: 6.00. Thanks.

2 A: Excuse me. Can you tell me (3) _____ we can go inside the palace?
   B: Yes, you can. It costs £12 a ticket.
   A: OK, can we have two tickets, please?
   B: Certainly. That's £24. Thank you. (4) _____ the palace.

3 A: Do you know (5) _____ we can take photos of the paintings?
   B: Here in the gallery?
   A: Yes.
   B: No, you can't. There's a (6) _____ that says 'no photography'.
   A: Oh yes.

4 A: Excuse me, do you know where the (7) _____ tube station is?
   B: Yeah, go out of the park.
   A: Yes.
   B: Through the gardens. And it's (8) _____ five minutes' walk.
   A: Out of the park and about five minutes.
   B: That's right.
   A: Thanks.

5 A: Can you tell me (9) _____ a 'chicken faal' is?
   B: It's a chicken dish. Very very hot.
   A: Oh really?
   B: Very spicy. But delicious.
   A: OK, I'll (10) _____ it.
   B: One chicken faal. Anything to drink?

6 A: Excuse me, do you know when the next train (11) _____ for Heathrow?
   B: Yes, you want the Heathrow Express. They leave every thirty minutes.
   A: Which platform?
   B: I don't know. You can ask (12) _____ there.
   A: Thank you very much.

c Listen and check your answers.

Reading

4 a Read the text. Mark the sentences true (T) or false (F).

1 Only the English and Japanese drive on the left.
2 England and the United Kingdom are the same.
3 The English are good at writing rules for sports.
4 In Britain there are people from many different countries.

b Tick (✓) the correct meaning of the words.

1 *head* (n)
   a person in control or at the top ☐
   b person who works at night ☐
2 *inhabitants* (n)
   a people who live in a place ☐
   b people from the UK ☐

FOUR THINGS YOU DIDN'T KNOW ABOUT ENGLAND

WHY DO THE ENGLISH DRIVE ON THE LEFT?

In the 1700s people used their right hand to carry a sword. But Napoleon carried his sword in his left hand and rode on the right. Everyone followed Napoleon because he ruled half the world. These days about 25% of countries still drive on the left, including Japan and the West Indies.

Top tip: Don't forget to drive on the left in the UK!

WHAT'S THE DIFFERENCE BETWEEN ENGLAND AND THE UNITED KINGDOM?

England is one country. The United Kingdom is England, Scotland, Wales and Northern Ireland (the Republic of Ireland, in the south, is an independent country.) The Prime Minister is the head of all four of these countries.

Top tip: Never say, 'You're English, aren't you?' to someone from Scotland, Ireland or Wales.

DO THE ENGLISH REALLY LOVE SPORT?

The English invented many of the world's most popular sports. They wrote the rules for football, boxing, tennis, cricket and many more. Unfortunately, the English are better at writing rules than winning games.

Top tip: Don't ask someone from England when England last won a football competition.

HOW MULTICULTURAL IS BRITAIN?

Britain is one of the world's most multicultural countries. You can hear hundreds of languages in London alone. In fact, 15% of the UK's 56 million inhabitants were born outside the UK.

Top tip: Visit the Notting Hill carnival in late August. It is two days of multicultural music, food and dancing.

Vocabulary | stages of life

1 Find nine words connected with times of life and write them below. Write (n) if the word is a noun and (adj) for an adjective.

teenagerelderlymiddle-agedbabyoldchildadulttoddlerpensioner

2 Complete each sentence with one word. Write the words in the crossword.

Across

3 Doctors and lawyers earn a good _____ in my country. (Mohamed, Egypt)

5 You can learn to _____ a car when you are 17. (Mick, the UK)

7 Women usually _____ married in their late 30s. (Inge, Norway)

8 Most women _____ children in their 20s. (Nobantu, Malawi)

9 Most people _____ when they are 65. (Dave, the US)

Down

1 It's expensive to get a _____ of your own. (Thais, Brazil)

2 We _____ from university in our 20s. (Laura, Ireland)

4 Grandparents often _____ after the kids. (Romina, Italy)

6 Not many children _____ against their parents. (Jose, Spain)

Grammar | *should(n't), can('t) and (don't) have to*

3 a Read what four people say about their jobs. Use the verbs in brackets once each to complete the sentences.

Diane

(don't have to / can't / have to)

1 Most people _____ afford my designs.

2 I _____ attend all the fashion shows, but I do because I enjoy them.

3 I _____ work hard before Fashion Week in October. There are many things to do.

Clive

(don't have to / shouldn't / can)

4 We _____ smoke or drink, but some of us do after the match.

5 We _____ go to the gym but we go sometimes.

6 You _____ earn a lot of money if you play for the national team.

Rafael

(can't / have to / should)

7 I _____ take long holidays because the company needs me in the office.

8 I _____ speak to all my workers but I don't always have time.

9 I _____ make important business decisions.

Siegfried

(have to / shouldn't / should)

10 I tell people that they _____ eat too much sugar.

11 I tell people that they _____ visit me three times a year.

12 I _____ look into people's mouths every day.

b What jobs do they do? Choose from the words in the box.

> dentist lawyer businessman actress
> doctor singer gardener fashion designer
> journalist taxi driver teacher footballer

1 Diane _____

2 Clive _____

3 Rafael _____

4 Siegfried _____

4 Correct the sentences by crossing out one word.

1 I can't be look after the children today.
2 Do you have not to work at weekends?
3 Should we to go to the shop this morning?
4 I am have to buy a new guitar.
5 I can to swim very well.
6 You shouldn't of play there. It's dangerous.
7 Can you will help me with my bags?
8 I don't have not to do any homework tonight.

5 Choose the correct words to complete the text.

Growing up in a big family

Liv Grundy has eighteen brothers and sisters.
There are good and bad things about living in a
big family. Money is always a problem. We (1) _____
afford holidays and we (2) _____ share bedrooms.
We are very close as a family. My parents (3) _____
look after all the children so the older ones help
the younger ones. I wash my younger brothers' clothes.
Families (4) _____ eat together every day but we
don't. We usually eat in two shifts (ten of us at
6.30, the rest at 7.30.) We (5) _____ buy a lot of
food, of course.
People ask us things like, '(6) _____ you
remember the names of all your brothers and
sisters?' Of course I can. And they ask, 'Do you
buy everyone presents at Christmas?' The answer
is no, we (7) _____. Christmas (8) _____ be just
about presents.

1 A don't have to   B haven't
  C can't   D should
2 A have to   B should
  C can   D don't
3 A can't   B should
  C have   D can
4 A doesn't have to   B can't
  C don't   D should
5 A shouldn't   B has to
  C have to   D don't have to
6 A Can   B Have
  C Should   D Have to
7 A should   B can
  C doesn't have to   D don't have to
8 A should   B can
  C shouldn't   D don't have to

Pronunciation

6 a [5.1] Underline the words you hear.

1 You *should/shouldn't* go home.
2 We *can/can't* see very well.
3 You *have to/don't have to* do the shopping.
4 *Can/Can't* you read?
5 We *should/shouldn't* watch this.
6 I *have to/don't have to* work tonight.
7 *Should/Shouldn't* he call me?
8 I *can/can't* understand it.
9 They *have to/don't have to* come.

b Listen and repeat the sentences.

How to ...

7 a Put the words in order to complete the sentences.

1 A: _____ (my in opinion),
   you need a haircut.
   B: _____. (think don't so I)

2 A: _____? (do think you what)
   B: You look interesting.

3 A: We need to clean this room.
   B: _____. (right you're probably)

4 A: Beautiful scenery. _____?
   (think you so don't)
   B: _____. (not sure so I'm)

b [5.2] Listen and check your answers.

Reading

1 **a** Read the texts. Write C (Carnegie), S (Soros), CS (both of them) or N (neither of them).

1 Who left his country when he was a teenager? __
2 Who had a good education? __
3 Which of them made his money in the US? __
4 Which of them worked in politics? __
5 Who created new institutions to help people? __
6 Who gave money to improve education? __
7 Who returned to his home country to live? __
8 Who wrote books? __

b Find words 1–4 in the text. Match them to the correct definitions (a–d) below.

1 invest in (v) (*line 10*) __
2 charity (n) (*line 14*) __
3 institution (n) (*line 27*) __
4 human rights (n) (*line 29*) __

a a big organisation
b put money into a business
c an organisation that gives money or things to people who need help
d things that everyone should be free to do/have

Friends of the World

¹ Andrew Carnegie
Andrew Carnegie was born in Scotland in 1835. His family was very poor. When Carnegie was 13 years old the
⁵ family moved to Pittsburgh in the US. He didn't finish his education, but a rich man called James Anderson gave Carnegie books from his library. As a young man, Carnegie worked
¹⁰ on the railway. He invested his money in business and made money quickly. In 1873 he started his own steel company. By 1900 the company was producing 25% of the steel in the US. There were no free public libraries in the US so Carnegie built 2,800 of them. He also gave a lot of money to charity.
¹⁵ Finally he returned to Scotland, where he wrote several books. He gave away 90% of his money and died in 1919.

George Soros
George Soros was born in Budapest, Hungary, in 1930. An intelligent young man, Soros went to England in 1947 and studied at the
²⁰ London School of Economics. Nine years later he went to the US. Soros started an international investment company and became rich

quickly. He understood international financial markets, and was called, 'the man who broke the Bank of England' when, in 1992, he earned $1.1 billion in one day.
Soros created institutions to solve world problems in health, education, the media and human rights. These institutions cost $400 million a year. Soros now writes books about politics, economics and society.

Grammar | Present Perfect with *for* and *since*

2 One ending is not possible. Cross it out.

1 I haven't been to the cinema *for ages/since June/since years*.

2 We haven't played tennis *since last year/ages ago/for months*.

3 She's worked here *for two weeks/since three months/ for a long time*.

4 I've played the piano *since I was a child/since ages/for five years*.

5 Have you lived here *for a long time/since January/ years ago*?

6 Has she known him *for years/since last July/for February*.

7 I haven't seen you *since I was in India/for a year or two/since months*.

8 He's been in the team *since two weeks/since he scored his first goal/for too long*.

3 Write sentences with the same meaning. Use the words in brackets. Write 2–5 words.

1 I arrived in China last Thursday. (here)

I've been _____ Thursday.

2 It is 2005. She first lived here in 2000. (lived)

She _____ five years.

3 I met John at school. He's my best friend. (known)

I've _____ we were at school.

4 Letitia doesn't smoke. She stopped years ago. (hasn't)

Letitia _____ years.

5 I last saw Giorgio seven days ago. (haven't)

I _____ last week.

6 I first played tennis in 1990 and I still play now. (have)

I _____ 1990.

7 We arrived at 6.00 a.m. and it's now 9.00 a.m.! (been)

We _____ three hours!

8 I'm a poet. I wrote my first poem years ago. (poetry)

I've _____ a long time.

4 Complete the dialogues. Use the Present Perfect form of the verbs in brackets.

1 A: How long _____ (they/live) here?

B: Twenty-four hours!

2 A: When did he arrive?

B: _____ (he/be) here all evening.

3 A: Cigarette?

B: No, thanks. _____ (I/not smoke) for years.

4 A: Where are the dogs?

B: I don't know. _____ (I/not see) them for ages.

5 A: How long _____ (you/know) him?

B: Since school.

6 A: Nice hairstyle!

B: _____ (she/have) it for years.

7 A: Is Gregor coming?

B: I don't know. _____ (we/not speak) to him for weeks.

8 A: How long _____ (he/wear) that suit?

B: Since I met him, ten years ago!

Vocabulary | friendship

5 Choose the correct word or words to complete the text.

From: h.pataudi@pashmina.com
To: will.greenwood@yakso.co.uk
Subject: hi

Dear Will,
Great to hear from you. I was worried I don't want to (1)_____ with you.
I'm very well. I've got a new girlfriend! I met (2)_____ a few weeks ago and he introduced me to his friend, Kim. Now I'm (3)_____ her! I met her parents and I (4)_____ with them.
Work is fine. I share an office with two (5)_____, Mary and Kunle. They are really nice.
Anyway, when you next visit Manchester, (6)_____.
All the best,
Hanif

1 A lose touch B miss touch C stop touch

2 A best friends B an old school friend
  C a girlfriend

3 A going on B going out C going out with

4 A got on well B got in C got over

5 A work people B work friends
  C colleagues

6 A get on touch B come in touch
  C get in touch

Writing

6 Add punctuation and capital letters to the text.

since university ive worked as a sales representative for a publishing company its a nice job my colleagues are really friendly and i travel a lot at the moment im living in milan i've been here two years and i love the city im not married i havent been in touch with anyone from university for years but id love to hear from you so send me an email sandy smith

Reading and listening

1 **a** [5.3] Read or listen to the text and choose the best title.

- Ten Ways to Live Happily
- A Long, Long Life
- Jean Calment's Lawyer

Jeanne Calment was born in 1875 and died in 1997. At 122 years old, she was the world's oldest person.

She was born in Arles and became a celebrity in her **home town**. Journalists asked her about the secrets of her **long life**. She told them she used to eat chocolate, put olive oil on her skin, **smoke two cigarettes a day** and drink red wine. But the truth, her doctor said, is that she never **felt stressed**. She once said, 'If you can't do anything about it, why worry about it?' She also had a good **sense of humour**. When one visitor said to her, 'Maybe see you next year,' she replied, 'I don't see why not. You don't look so bad to me.'

She used to **ride a bike** (she stopped when she was 100), and her mind was strong even after her body **grew old**. She said, 'I never **get bored**.'

The best **true Calment story** was about her house. When she was 90, her lawyer bought the house. He paid her only $400 a month, a very small **amount of money**. His plan was to get the house when Jeanne Calment died. But he died first, aged 77, after paying $180,000, much more than the house was worth!

b Cover the text. Match a word from A to a word from B to make phrases from the text.

A
home   long   smoke
drink   feel   sense of
ride   grow   get
true   amount of

B
cigarettes   humour
money   old   a bike
wine   town   stressed
bored   story   life

c Use the phrases in Ex. 1b to complete the summary. You may need to change the verb form.

1 She is famous because she lived a _____ _____.
2 She died in her _____ _____, Arles.
3 She _____ two _____ a day and _____ red _____.
4 She never _____ _____.
5 She had a good _____ _____ _____.
6 She _____ _____ _____ until she was 100.
7 Her mind stayed young even when her body _____ _____.
8 There is a funny _____ _____ about her house and her lawyer.
9 Her lawyer thought he would pay her a small _____ _____ _____ for the house. He was wrong!

Grammar | *used to*

2 **a** Write *Yes/No* questions using *used to* and the prompts.

play/any instruments
Did you use to play any instruments?

1 watch/a lot of TV
_____?

2 go abroad/for your holidays
_____?

3 cook/for your parents
_____?

4 help your mother/around the house
_____?

5 do/a lot of exercise
_____?

b Match the questions (1–6) to the answers.
a Yes, I always washed the dishes.
b No, I hated sport.
c Yes, I went to Jamaica, India . . .
d No. My father used to make the dinner.
e Yes, four hours every day.

3 Correct the sentences by adding or crossing out one word.

1 Did you use work here?
2 I used always to eat junk food.
3 Didn't she to be a singer?
4 She didn't use to be smoke so much.
5 Did use to get on well with your grandparents?
6 We were used to have to work all the time.
7 I didn't use listen to the radio.
8 We used then to have a house on the beach.

Listening

4 **a** `5·4` Listen and complete the table. The first one has been done for you.

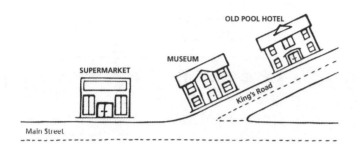

IS NOW	USED TO BE
A supermarket	a school
B car park	_____
C museum	_____
D Old Pool Hotel	_____

b Listen again and complete the sentences with the missing words or phrases.

A: It's changed a lot. This is Main Street, the biggest street in town. You see the supermarket on the left here?

B: Yes.

A: This (1) _____ a school.

B: Really?

A: Yes, it was my school. But about ten years ago they closed it. Now it's a supermarket.

B: I see.

A: On the right here, you see the car park?

B: Yes.

A: There (2) _____ a car park here. It was a sports field. We played football here every day.

B: A sports field?

A: That's right.

B: Where are we now?

A: This is King's Road. The museum (3) _____ the hospital.

B: Really?

A: It was called King's Hospital. They built the museum about ten years ago.

B: What type of museum is it?

A: Art. It's got a lot of old art.

B: Old Pool Hotel. Didn't there (4) _____ a swimming pool here?

A: Yes, there did. There weren't any tourists in the past.

B: So the hotel used to be the swimming pool?

A: Yes.

B: Did you use to come here when you were young?

A: No, I (5) _____ . I preferred the sea.

Pronunciation

5 `5·5` Listen and repeat the sentences.
1 This used to be a school.
2 There didn't use to be a car park.
3 The museum used to be a hospital.
4 I used to come here to study.
5 Did there use to be a swimming pool?
6 There didn't use to be a hotel.

Vocabulary | good and bad habits

6 Complete the sentences and write the words in the puzzle. Find the key word.

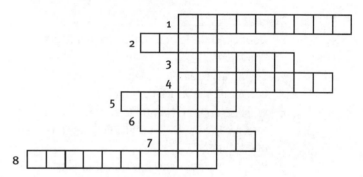

1 **A:** Do you always eat good food, like fruit and vegetables?
   B: Yes. I like to eat _____ly.
2 **A:** Do you always eat hamburgers, chips and chocolate?
   B: Yes. I love eating junk f_____!
3 **A:** Do you smoke forty cigarettes a day?
   B: Yes. I'm a heavy _____r.
4 **A:** Do you go to the gym every day?
   B: Yes. I love doing _____al exercise.
5 **A:** Do you like reading, playing chess and doing crosswords?
   B: Yes. I like to be mentally a_____.
6 **A:** Do you always go to bed at 3 a.m.?
   B: Yes. I go to bed very l_____.
7 **A:** Do you always carry bottles in your bag?
   B: Yes. I drink a lot of w_____.
8 **A:** Do you always feel good about life?
   B: Yes. I always think p_____y.

Vocabulary | geography

1 Answer the questions below to complete the crossword.

Down

1 Quebec, Ontario and British Columbia are all regions of _____.
3 The Algarve region is a popular tourist destination in which country?
5 Which European country is surrounded by Austria, the Czech Republic, Poland, Ukraine and Hungary?
8 Which continent now has 22 countries?
9 What is the capital of Egypt?

Across

2 In which country are the remains of the ancient city of Pompeii?
4 Lake Geneva is situated in south-west _____.
6 In which Asian country is Mount Fuji situated?
7 Which nationality of people started the Olympic Games?
10 The Black Forest is in which country?
11 What nationality was the painter Pablo Picasso?
12 Which language do people speak in Brazil?

2 Use the words in the box to complete the sentences.

> sea   mountain   lake   beaches   island
> ocean   river   forest   desert

1 Australia is the biggest _____ in the world.
2 The Pacific is the largest _____ in the world.
3 The Nile is the longest _____ in the world.
4 The highest _____ in the Alps is Mont Blanc.
5 The mountains of Canada are covered in a thick _____.
6 The long, white _____ in Brazil are beautiful.
7 Over 80% of the country of Egypt is a _____.
8 The Caspian Sea is surrounded by land so it is, in fact, the world's biggest _____.
9 The city of Odessa, Ukraine, is on the coast of the Black _____.

Grammar | will

3 Complete the dialogues using *will* or *won't* and a verb from the box.

> know   be   pay   carry   sleep   show

1 **A:** This bag is very heavy!
   B: Let me help. I _____ it for you.
2 **A:** Shall we talk about this tomorrow?
   B: No. I _____ here tomorrow.
3 **A:** I don't have any money for the taxi.
   B: It's alright. I _____ for it.
4 **A:** Would you like some coffee?
   B: No, thanks. I _____ tonight if I drink it now.
5 **A:** How does this computer work?
   B: Come here and I _____ you.
6 **A:** How were your exam results?
   B: I _____ until I go back to school.

4 Choose the correct alternative.

1 I am going out to lunch. *I see you/I'll see you* later.

2 The weather is getting better. I think *I'll go/I go* to the beach this weekend.

3 *Will you stay/Do you stay* in the same hotel when you come back next month?

4 I am very tired. *I'll finish/I finish* this report tomorrow.

5 Is that the phone ringing? *I'll get/I get* it.

6 I love sport. *I do/I'll do* lots of sport at the weekends.

7 My mother is in hospital, so *I visit/I'll visit* her every day.

8 I haven't spoken to Jenny for ages. *I send/I'll send* her a postcard.

Pronunciation

5 **6.1** Do the underlined words in the story have the sound /ɒ/ or /əʊ/? Write the words in the table. Listen and check.

A man went to a sh<u>o</u>p to buy a dress for his wife. But when he got there the shop was cl<u>o</u>sed. 'I'm s<u>o</u>rry,' said the sh<u>o</u>pkeeper, 'but we close at five.' 'Oh dear,' said the man. 'My cl<u>o</u>ck st<u>o</u>pped, and now I'm late, and I have n<u>o</u> present for my wife.' 'D<u>o</u>n't worry,' said the sh<u>o</u>pkeeper. 'I'll <u>o</u>pen the shop for you. But <u>o</u>nly if you pr<u>o</u>mise to buy the m<u>o</u>st expensive dress we have g<u>o</u>t!' The man did this and went home. He didn't kn<u>o</u>w that the shopkeeper's clock always said 5.05 pm.

/ɒ/ orange	/əʊ/ won't

Reading

6 **a** You are going to read about two tourist destinations: Switzerland and Western Australia. Before you read, answer the questions. Write S if you think the answer is Switzerland or write WA if you think the answer is Western Australia.

Where

1 do people speak different languages in the different cities?

2 can you explore the desert?

3 can you find beautiful beaches?

4 can you visit lakes in the mountains?

5 can you swim with dolphins?

b Read the texts to check your answers.

Switzerland is (1) *one of Europe's most* beautiful countries. Cities like Zurich seem like a concrete jungle, and then you look up and see the wonderful mountains of the Alps. (2) *In the north* the landscape has a natural beauty, with green fields and villages which look like the pictures on a chocolate box. Each of Switzerland's main cities has a different character, from French-speaking Geneva to German Bern to Italian Lugano. Swiss people (3) *are famous for* their efficiency, so travelling around the country is easy. Switzerland's beautiful lakes, clean air, and fields full of flowers (4) *attract visitors throughout the year.*

Western Australia

Sun, adventure, a beautiful environment and friendly people. This is what you'll find on a holiday to Western Australia.
Western Australia has a natural beauty, long days of sunshine, clear blue skies, and fantastic beaches. (5) *Come to Western Australia to* swim with wild dolphins, walk through the ancient forest, or sleep under the stars in the Outback desert. (6) *Why not start your holiday* in the capital city of Western Australia, Perth? You can spend an afternoon sitting outside a pub and enjoying a cool drink with the locals.

7 Mark these sentences true (T), false (F) or no information (NI).

Switzerland

1 The north is more beautiful than the south.

2 The main language in Bern is German.

3 It's difficult to travel from one city to another city.

Western Australia

4 *Outback* is a town.

5 Perth is the capital of Western Australia.

6 There are a lot of pubs.

8 Phrases 1–6 in the text are useful ways of describing a tourist destination. Match 1–6 to a similar phrase (a–f) below.

a It's a good idea to start your holiday ...

b well-known because of

c In the south/east/west ...

d Visit ... in order to ...

e There are some very famous/beautiful/ expensive places. This is one of them.

f tourists like to visit this place all year

Grammar | *too/enough/many*

1 Complete the sentences using *too, too much, too many* or *enough*.

1 It's _____ crowded for me in the city. I prefer the country.

2 There are _____ people on the beach today.

3 There aren't _____ buses. We always have to wait.

4 There is _____ noise in here. I'm going to work next door.

5 It's _____ hot in the office. Can you turn on the air-conditioning?

6 I'm sorry, but I didn't have _____ money to buy you a drink.

7 I have got _____ homework to do. I'll never finish by tomorrow!

8 There are _____ TV channels. I can never decide which one to watch.

2 Look at the pictures. Complete the sentences using *too* or *enough* and words from the box.

> suitcases crowded loud money small tall

1 The music is _____ _____.

2 He isn't _____ _____.

3 They have got _____ many _____.

4 He hasn't got _____ _____ to buy food.

5 The train is _____ _____.

6 His jacket is _____ _____ for him.

3 Complete the sentences using *too, enough, too many, too much* and the words in brackets.

1 I'm not going to play football tonight. I'm _____ _____. (tired)

2 You are not working _____. You won't pass your exams. (hard)

3 He spends _____ on the computer. He never goes out. (time)

4 We would like to buy a new car, but it is _____ _____. (expensive)

5 Those children eat _____ . It's not good for them. (hamburgers)

6 I want to write to them in Russian, but my Russian is not _____. (good)

7 The film was really boring. It was _____. (long)

8 We didn't go into the museum, because there were _____. (people)

9 I can't speak to her now. I am _____. (busy)

10 You can't come into this club. You are not _____ _____. (old)

Vocabulary | machines at home

4 Use the pictures to complete the sentences.

1 Sorry I didn't call you earlier, but I couldn't find my _____.

2 I need to clean my house but my _____ isn't working.

3 Come and listen to my music. I've got a new _____.

4 You should put that ice cream in the _____ before it melts.

5 I left a message on your _____.

6 I heard an interesting programme on the _____ this morning.

7 Your hair is still wet. Do you want to use my _____?

8 You don't need to wash the dishes. We've got a _____.

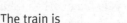
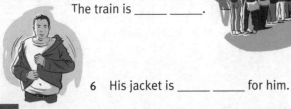
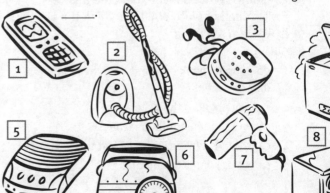

How to ...

5 Choose the correct alternative.

1 I think we *should/would* take the digital camera *because/so* it's better.

2 I *like/'d like* to take the CD player. I *couldn't/mustn't* live without it!

3 We'd like *choose/to choose* Istanbul for the new office. The *main/mains* reason is that it is a busy city.

4 I think we should *take/to take* a taxi to the airport. I'm *so/too* lazy to carry these bags on the train.

5 We think we should *go/to go* to the hotel first *because/because of* the restaurant is a long way from here.

Listening

6 **a** `6.2` Cover the tapescript. Listen to the conversation about a TV show and choose the best description.

1 *Amish in the City* takes five teenagers from an Amish community, who know nothing about technology, and moves them to live with other teenagers in Los Angeles. They are going to learn about modern life in Los Angeles.

2 *Amish in the City* takes five Los Angeles teenagers to a community of Amish people, where they learn how to live without modern technology. There are no cars, no mobile phones and there is no TV.

b Complete the tapescript using words from the box.

television   programme   teenagers
mobile telephones   interesting   car parks
confusing   technology

TAPESCRIPT

Woman: Have you seen that programme *Amish in the City*?

Man: No. Why?

Woman: Oh. It's really (1)_____. It's about these five Amish people. You know, they are these religious communities who live in America, in the countryside, and they don't have (2)_____.

Man: No technology? Don't they have computers?

Woman: No. Nothing. They build their own houses, and ride horses. They don't have cars, or (3)_____ or anything.

Man: Wow. So what happens in the (4)_____?

Woman: Well, the programme takes five Amish teenagers to live in a big house in Los Angeles, with some other (5)_____, who are not Amish.

Man: So the Los Angeles kids teach these Amish people about the modern world?

Woman: Yes. That's right. The Amish have never seen (6)_____ before, or CD players, videos , washing machines. Nothing!

Man: They have never seen them?

Woman: No. And they go to the beach, and the Amish have never seen the ocean before. It's really good.

Man: Yes, it sounds interesting.

Woman: They go out to discos, and go shopping.

Man: And do the Amish like what they see? Do they like the modern world?

Woman: Well, they find it very (7)_____. They don't know what to think. The girls like wearing the new clothes. And everything is very interesting for them, even things like (8)_____!

Man: Car parks? Do they ...

Grammar | *like/would like/be like/look like*

1 Choose the correct alternative.

1 A: *Do you like/Would you like* a glass of water?
   B: Yes, please.

2 A: *Do you like/Would you like* chocolate?
   B: Yes, I eat it every day.

3 A: Are you free this afternoon? Nadia *would like/likes* to meet you for a coffee.
   B: Yes. Tell her I can meet her at 4 p.m.

4 A: What time *do you like/would you like* to leave?
   B: Let's leave at 6.30 p.m.

5 A: *Do you like/Would you like* going out in the evening?
   B: Yes, but I don't stay out late.

6 A: Do you have Phil's email address? *I like/I'd like* to write to him, but I don't have his address here.
   B: Yes. It's Philip.Denton@aoi.com

2 **a** Complete the text using words from the box.

> like 'd like likes look like
> don't like 's he like am I like

My brother and I are twins, but we're very different. We don't (1)_____ each other because Marc is dark and I am blond, and we (2)_____ the same things. We eat different kinds of food, see different friends, and have different interests. He (3)_____ playing football, but I prefer reading books. I (4)_____ going out to parties but he prefers to stay at home and watch sport on TV. What (5)_____? Well, he's a great sportsman, but he's not very friendly. And what (6)_____? I have lots of friends but I am terrible at sport! I (7)_____ to be better at sport, but I think it is too late now. I'm nearly 40!

b Look at the pictures. Which man is the speaker? Which is Marc?

3 Choose the correct alternative.

1 Your eyes *look like/like/would like* Amanda's. Are you two sisters?

2 Do you *would like/like/are like* living in Spain?

3 *Would you like/Do you like/Are you like* to come to lunch with us?

4 A: I painted my new flat yesterday.
   B: Really? What *would you/does it look/do you look* like?

5 A: I prefer the old part of the city.
   B: Why? What *would you/is it look/is it* like?

6 A: *Would you/Do you/Are you* like a drink?
   B: Thank you. I *like/'d like/look like* an orange juice.

7 A: I don't know Marek. What *does he look/is he look/would he* like?
   B: He's tall, with dark hair and very blue eyes.

8 A: *Would you like/Do you like/Are you like* cooking?
   B: Yes. I love it.

9 A: What *is/does/looks* your new teacher like?
   B: She is really good. I like her.

10 A: You've been to Tunisia. *What do you/What's it/What would you* like?
    B: It's very hot, and the people are very friendly.

Pronunciation

4 **a** **6.3** Cover the tapescript. Listen and write the questions.

b Underline the stressed words.

c Practise saying the questions.

> **TAPESCRIPT**
> 1 What do you like doing at the weekend?
> 2 What would you like to do this evening?
> 3 What's your mother like?
> 4 What does she look like?
> 5 Do you like swimming?
> 6 Would you like some help?

Reading and listening

5 a **6.4** Read and listen to the story.

The Richest Man in the World by Ferenc Sjorzsinskev

He sat in his garden, drinking coffee. On the sofa behind him there was a washing machine, and on the washing machine a video player, a vacuum cleaner and an old radio. Next to the sofa there was a fridge with a hairdryer on top of it. And as the sun got higher and hotter, he just sat there on his chair drinking coffee.

It was Sunday and there were families walking back from church. One old couple saw him and stopped.

'Hello there!' said the old man.

'Good morning,' said the man on the chair.

The old couple stood <u>there</u>.

'Mr,' said the old man. 'We . . . er . . . we see you have a washing machine.'

'That's right,' said the man drinking coffee.

'Er . . . is it a sale? I mean, do you want to sell <u>it</u>?'

'A sale? I wouldn't say that exactly.'

'Because we would like to buy that washing machine, you see.'

'OK,' said the man. 'How much do you want to pay?'

The old man said, 'I only have ten dollars on me at the moment.'

'Ten dollars?'

The old man put his hand in his pocket and pulled out some coins, some paper, a bag of tobacco.

'I know <u>it</u>'s not enough, but I can get more. I can go home and get you more money, or we can wait till tomorrow when the bank is open . . .'

'Ten dollars?' said the man drinking coffee. He put the cup down. 'Ten dollars is too much. I'll sell it to you for two dollars fifty.'

The old couple looked at each other. And they bought the washing machine for two dollars fifty cents, and they called their sons, who lived with them, and the sons carried the washing machine away.

A little later, a young family came to the garden. They looked at the man and the man looked at them: five children, no shoes, one dog on a string.

'What's your dog's name?' said the man.

The youngest boy shouted, 'Loopy! <u>His</u> name's Loopy!'

The boy dropped the string and Loopy walked across the garden, his nose to the ground. He came to the sofa and smelled the ghosts of other dogs.

'Hey, Mr,' said the young woman. 'Are you selling that fridge?'

'Yes, I am. But it'll cost you.'

'How much?'

'Two dollars. And if that's too much, I'll take one fifty.'

And the mother bought the fridge for one dollar and twelve cents and the children picked <u>it</u> up and carried it home, all except the youngest boy who ran with the dog on a string.

A little later, the man sold his video player to a young couple for ten cents. Then he sold his hairdryer to an old lady with blue hair. Then finally he even sold the sofa. Now, in the early evening, there was nothing in his garden except the last heat of the sun and a small breath of wind in the man's face.

The boy with the dog on a string came back.

'Hello, Loopy!' said the man.

'Can I ask you something, Mr?'

'Of course you can.'

'Mr, are you rich?'

The man smiled. He looked at the first stars shining and a big lemon moon behind a tree. He had eight dollars and seventy cents in his hand.

'Yes,' he said. 'I'm the richest man in the world.'

b Correct the sentences to make a summary of the story.

1 A man was drinking coffee in his house.
2 A young couple walked past and asked if they could buy his washing machine.
3 The old man only had $5.
4 They bought the dishwasher for $2.50.
5 Later, the man sold his fridge to a family with six children and a dog.
6 Then he sold his computer, his hairdryer and his sofa.
7 He had $870.
8 When a young boy returned with his dog, the old man told him that he was the happiest man in the world.

Writing

6 a Find these <u>underlined</u> words in the text. What do they refer to?

1 there (*line 10*)
2 it (*line 13*)
3 it (*line 21*)
4 his (*line 31*)
5 it (*line 39*)

b Rewrite the second sentences using referencing words.

1 The painting was hanging on the wall. The painting was beautiful.

_____

2 Kiev is a beautiful city. The people who live in Kiev are lucky.

_____

3 The lake is so pretty in the summer. I love watching the lake.

_____

4 The desert was very quiet. It felt like we were the only people in the desert.

_____

Comparatives and superlatives

1 Complete the sentences using the adjectives in brackets. Use a comparative or superlative.

1 Malawi is _____ (hot) than Iceland.

2 Wolves are _____ (dangerous) than dogs.

3 Elephants are _____ (large) land mammals in the world.

4 Russ is _____ (young) than me.

5 The Psychology course is _____ (interesting) the History course.

6 *Casablanca* is _____ (romantic) film I've ever seen.

7 The Karoo Desert is _____ (small) than the Sahara.

8 That was _____ (good) day of my life.

9 Sarah is _____ (lazy) than her sister.

10 Hannah bought _____ (pretty) dress in the shop.

11 My old teacher was _____ (kind) than the new one.

12 He's _____ (fast) runner in our team.

Indirect questions

2 Make the questions indirect.

When does the library open?
Can you tell me when the library opens?

1 What time does the bus leave?
Can you tell . . .

2 How much do these shoes cost?
Can you tell . . .

3 Who was the 41st US President?
Do you know . . .

4 How does this photocopier work?
Can you tell me . . .

5 What is the capital of Mexico?
Do you know . . .

6 When does the next train leave?
Do you know . . .

7 Is the museum open on Sundays?
Can you tell . . .

8 Is there a train to Asiago?
Do you know . . .

9 Does Josh work here?
Can you tell . . .

10 Do penguins fly?
Do you know . . .

should(n't), can('t), (don't) have to

3 Make sentences with the same meaning. Use the words in brackets. Write 2–3 words.

1 I know how to fly an aeroplane.
I _____ an aeroplane. (can)

2 It's a good idea to buy our tickets early.
We _____ our tickets early. (should)

3 It isn't necessary to pay for children.
You _____ pay for children. (have)

4 She needs to do her exam again.
She _____ her exam again. (has)

5 Is it possible for me to go home now?
_____ home now? (Can)

6 It's not a good idea to arrive late.
We _____ late. (shouldn't)

7 She doesn't know how to drive.
She _____ . (can't)

8 Is it necessary to read this book?
Do we _____ this book? (have)

9 It's healthy to eat more vegetables.
You _____ more vegetables. (should)

10 Is it necessary for me to leave?
Do _____ leave?

used to and Present Perfect with for and since

4 Complete the gaps with *used to* and the words in brackets. Then match to a–e and choose *for* or *since*.

1 I _____ (smoke)

2 She _____ (be) good at the guitar

3 We _____ (not/like) each other when we were children

4 Mum and Dad _____ (travel) a lot

5 I _____ (not/cook) much pasta

a but we've been friends *for / since* the last few months.

b but I've eaten a lot of it *for / since* I went to Italy.

c but I haven't had a cigarette *for / since* last year.

d but they haven't had a holiday *for / since* 1999.

e but she hasn't played *for / since* two years.

42

will with *too/enough/very*

5 Make predictions using *will*/*won't* and circle the correct underlined word.

1 The disco _____ (be) full now. There are always *enough* /*too* many people.

2 Where _____ (you/have) breakfast? Jojo's Café serves *very* /*enough* good food.

3 She _____ (stay) in this hotel because it's *too* /*enough* expensive.

4 What time _____ (they/arrive)? Not *enough* /*very* late, I hope.

5 My new flat is *too* /*very* close to my office, so I _____ (need) to drive to work.

6 She _____ (study) law if her exam results are good *very* /*enough*.

7 It's *too* /*enough* cold to eat outside. Also, I think it _____ (rain) this afternoon.

8 It's a *very* /*too* short film, so we _____ (be) home late .

9 Where _____ (you/go) on your next holiday? Bali is beautiful and not *very* / *enough* expensive.

10 We _____ (go) swimming this afternoon because the water is *enough* /*too* cold.

like/would like/be like/look like

6 Put the words in order to make questions. Match the questions to the answers a–h.

1 you a Would like drink

   _____ ☐

2 she her sister look Does like

   _____ ☐

3 do in free What you doing like time your

   _____ ☐

4 is John's like What girlfriend

   _____ ☐

5 would go to Where you like tomorrow

   _____ ☐

6 you like Who look do

   _____ ☐

7 brother Does your like Ireland

   _____ ☐

8 book like is What that

   _____ ☐

a It's OK but the story is a bit boring.

b My father. We are both blond with blue eyes.

c Yes, he loves it, especially the people.

d Yes, they both have long red hair and green eyes.

e I like listening to music and playing with my dogs.

f She's really friendly and very intelligent.

g No thanks. I'm not thirsty.

h To the park. I want to see the birds.

Vocabulary

7 Write a word from Units 4, 5 or 6 in the gaps to match the definitions. The first letter of each word is supplied.

1 a_____ (*n*) not a child (Unit 5.0)

2 b_____ (*adj*) doesn't fear anything (4.1)

3 c_____ (*n*) something that is difficult to do (4.0)

4 d_____ (*n*) place with a lot of sand and not much water (6.1)

5 e_____ (*adj*) old (5.0)

6 f_____ (*n*) geographical feature with many big trees (6.1)

7 g_____ (*adj*) kind (4.1)

8 h_____ (*adv*) when you eat the right amount of good food, you eat . . . (5.3)

9 i_____ (*n*) not stupid (4.1)

10 j_____ (*adj*) . . . food = what you eat in fast food restaurants (5.3)

11 k_____ (*n*) first aid . . . = necessary to survive in the wild (4.4)

12 l_____ (*v*) . . . touch = not stay in contact (5.2)

13 m_____ (*adj*) not young or old (5.0)

14 n_____ (*n*) discos, bars etc. (6.4)

15 o_____ (*n*) very big sea (6.1)

16 p_____ (*n*) old person who doesn't worknow (5.0)

17 q_____ (*n*) they need answers (6.1)

18 r_____ (*v*) trust or depend on someone (4.0)

19 s_____ (*n*) a person who smokes (5.3)

20 t_____ (*adj*) has a lot of natural ability (4.1)

21 u_____ (*n*) it stops the rain from falling on your head (4.4)

22 v_____ (*n*) machine for recording and watching films (6.2)

23 w_____ (*n*) use it to clean clothes (6.2)

24 x_____ (*adj*) not old (5.0)

25 y_____ (*n*) New . . . = famous for sheep, rugby and Lord of the Rings (6.1)

Vocabulary | appearance

1 Put the letters in order to label the pictures.

1	twias _____	8	neke _____
2	dohulers _____	9	ginfre _____
3	blewo _____	10	hekec _____
4	stirw _____	11	lanek _____
5	rae _____	12	yee _____
6	seon _____	13	tumoh _____
7	kacb _____	14	ahri _____

2 Complete each sentence with one word.

1 I look _____ my mother because we both have the same eyes.

2 I shouldn't eat too much pasta or I will _____ on weight.

3 I am going _____ a diet but I'll start next week.

4 Working hard _____ me stressed.

5 She spends an hour in the bathroom every morning. Her physical _____ is very important to her.

Trisha's Wedding Day

3 **a** Complete the text using adjectives from the box.

> tall   skinny   handsome   medium height
> thin   good-looking   short   overweight
> muscular   well-built

Trisha: 'You can see my mother. She's the (1) _____ (not tall), slightly (2) _____ (a bit fat) lady on the left. And standing next to her is my father. He's very (3) _____ (not short) and (4) _____ (not fat)! There's my brother, Jake, at the back. He's very (5) _____ (big, but not fat) and (6) _____ (with big muscles). He's (7) _____ (not tall, not short), and that's his girlfriend next to him. She's a bit (8) _____ (too thin), if you ask me. And the (9) _____ (not short), (10) _____ (beautiful, male) man at the front is my new husband, Pierre. He's really (11) _____ (attractive physically), isn't he?'

b Choose the correct alternative.

1 He goes to the gym every day so he's very handsome / muscular / short.

2 My trousers are too small for me. I must be thin / medium height / overweight.

3 A: Do you think he's good-looking?
   B: Yes, I think he's handsome / skinny / tall.

4 Her mother is very short but she's quite tall / well-built / handsome.

5 I'm not tall and not short. I'm muscular / medium height / overweight.

6 I think you need to eat more. You're too overweight / tall / skinny.

4 a Which two letters make two words from the Lesson?

Example: f *a t* tractive (fat, attractive)

1 wai _ _ omach
2 mou _ _ in
3 wri _ _ ressed
4 handso _ _ dicine
5 sever _ _ ternative
6 ank _ _ ssons
7 sandwi _ _ eek
8 fa _ _ lebrity
9 mon _ _ umb

b Complete the sentences using words from Ex. 3a.

1 I am working too hard and I feel _____.
2 If you are feeling sick, you should take some _____.
3 I'm hungry. I'm going to make a cheese _____.
4 My trousers are too big. I need a belt to put around my _____.
5 I go out with colleagues from work about once a _____.
6 He's been very successful and now he is a _____.
7 If you want to read a book, there are _____ on the desk.
8 I am doing a massage course. My _____ start on Monday.

Grammar | first conditional

5 Complete the sentences with phrases from the box.

> we'll talk about it later.
> I'll buy you a copy for your birthday.
> we'll celebrate with a party.
> I'll go to the bank and get some.
> will you come?
> we'll stay in and eat a pizza.
> there won't be any left.

1 If you pass your exams, _____
2 If you don't want to go out tonight, _____
3 If you need some more money, _____
4 If you like that CD, _____
5 If you're too busy now, _____
6 If we don't buy tickets soon, _____
7 If I invite you to the party, _____

6 Choose the correct alternative.

1 If you *see/will see* Max, *will you/do you* tell him I want to talk to him?
2 If they *won't come/don't come* home soon, their dinner *will be/is* cold.
3 Your mother *will be/is* worried if you *don't call/won't call* her.
4 If you *don't leave/won't leave* now, *you'll miss/you miss* the train.
5 Your manager *won't be/is not* very happy if you *will go/go* to work in those clothes.
6 If we *find/will find* a nice restaurant, *we'll tell/we tell* you about it.
7 We*'ll be/are* in New York by 8 o'clock if there *aren't/won't be* any problems.
8 If you *don't sleep/won't sleep* well tonight, you *won't feel/do not feel* good in the morning.

7 Pete and Shaune are going to a health farm. Complete the sentences using the prompts.

1 If Pete / do / lots of exercise / his muscles / get stronger
_____
2 If Shaune / do yoga / she / feel happier
_____
3 Their / skin / look better / if they / drink / lots of water
_____
4 They / feel / more relaxed / if they / have / massages every day
_____
5 If Shaune / eat salads / for a week / she / lose weight
_____
6 They / not feel / so tired / if they / sleep / for ten hours a day
_____
7 If they / not smoke / for a week / they / feel healthier
_____
8 They / be / less stressed / if they / not think / about work
_____
9 If Pete / lose weight / he / have / more energy
_____

New Internet design company is looking for a young, (1) _____ (wants success) person to help us increase business in our second year.

Friendly, (2) _____ (easy to talk to and talks a lot) waitress needed for local café. Experience an advantage.

Nurses needed to help look after old people in their homes. You should be (3) _____ (good at planning and doing things you have to do) and (4) _____ (think about how other people will feel*).

We are looking for a new gardener. Must be (5) _____ (wants to work hard).

University library needs assistant. The job is good for a quiet, (8) _____ (does not talk about feelings) person.

Vocabulary | adjectives of personality

1 Complete the job adverts using words from the box. One of the words is not necessary.

> ambitious hard-working reserved sensitive
> open organised lazy unreliable chatty

Would you like to be on TV? Are you happy to talk about your relationships? We are looking for (6) _____ (happy to talk about feelings) people to be part of a new TV show. No (7) _____ (doesn't do what he/she should do) people, please.

* this word also means 'easily upset'

Pronunciation

2 **7.1** Listen to the pronunciation of the words from Ex. 1. Write them in the correct column of the table.

oOo	oO	Oo	Ooo
ambitious			

Grammar | gerund and infinitive

3 Choose the correct alternative.

1 She seemed *to think/thinking* that the concert was yesterday.

2 I've enjoyed *to talk/talking* to you.

3 We can't avoid *to meet/meeting* him.

4 He offered *to take/taking* us to the station.

5 I can't imagine *to work/working* without a computer.

6 I've decided *to change/changing* my job.

7 We considered *to move/moving* to the US.

8 They didn't expect *to find/finding* you here.

9 Do you promise not *to tell/telling* anyone?

10 I miss *to see/seeing* the mountains.

4 Complete the story using the correct form of the verbs in brackets.

You will have a long life.

When a woman read my palm, I didn't expect (1)_____ (learn) anything new. I don't believe in things like that and I avoid (2)_____ (look at) my horoscope. Then I met a woman in a bar who offered (3)_____ (read) my palm. At first I didn't want her (4)_____ (do) it, but then I decided (5)_____ (try) it. She promised not (6)_____ (tell) me anything terrible. She told me about the problems I had at work. She told me that I wanted (7)_____ (change) things. I really enjoyed (8)_____ (listen) to her and she seemed (9)_____ (understand) me. Then she told me I would go on a journey which would change my life. I laughed because I couldn't afford (10)_____ (travel). Two weeks later I won a holiday to the Caribbean. Can you imagine (11)_____ (win) a holiday like that? Anyway I met my husband on that holiday, so it really did change my life! I have always wanted (12)_____ (say) thank you to that woman in the bar.

5 There are mistakes in some of the sentences. Find the mistakes and correct them.

1 I am hoping to meeting the artist at the exhibition.

2 I miss to see my friends and family.

3 I expect you be here at 9 o'clock.

4 She offered to help me with the cooking.

5 He has decided taking a week off work.

6 We avoided to tell you earlier because of your exams.

7 You can't afford going out every night. It's too expensive.

8 I promised to going to her house this evening.

9 I want tell you what happened.

10 It seems to be the cheapest shop.

Reading

6 **a** Read the quiz and answer the questions. Then read about how your personality can help you learn English.

b Tick (✓) the correct answers.

1 According to the text, an extrovert enjoys

A walking alone.

B being with lots of different people.

C talking on the phone.

D making new friends.

E doing homework.

2 According to the text an introvert enjoys

A being at home with family and friends.

B sitting in the centre of a room.

C going to parties.

D talking to small groups of people.

E making mistakes.

---

1 **Do you make friends quickly when you start a new job?**
YES / NO

2 **Do you spend your free time going out, shopping and being with other people?**
YES / NO

3 **Are you usually the first person to answer the phone?**
YES / NO

4 **Do you have a lot of different friends?**
YES / NO

5 **Do you enjoy going for walks on your own?**
YES / NO

6 **Do you like spending your free time relaxing in a quiet, family atmosphere?**
YES / NO

7 **Do you like talking to people in small groups?**
YES / NO

8 **Do you usually sit nearer the side, not in the centre, of a room?**
YES / NO

Score

Give yourself one point for every Yes you answered for questions 1–4. Give yourself one point for every No you answered for questions 5–8.

Your total score: ___ points

If you scored between 1–4 points, you are an introvert.

You enjoy spending time on your own, or with people you know well. Your friends and family are very important to you too. You can improve your English by reading books, listening to songs, studying on your own and talking to a friend in English. And don't worry too much when you make mistakes!

If you scored between 5–8 points, you are an extrovert.

You are very active and enjoy spending your time with people, especially at parties. You like talking, but sometimes you need to stop and listen. You learn English well in big groups where you can talk to lots of people and have fun. But remember to do your homework!

How to ...

1 Read the jokes and put the words in order to complete the responses.

1 **A:** Doctor, Doctor, I think I need glasses.
You certainly do. This is a fish and chip shop!
B: (funny really that's) _____.

2 **A:** Doctor, Doctor, my son has eaten my pen. What should I do?
Use a pencil until I arrive.
B: (get I it don't) _____.

3 Doctor, Doctor, I've broken my arm in two places.
Well, don't go back there again then!
B: (funny that's very not) _____.

Vocabulary | illness and injury

2 Use a word from A and a word from B to complete the sentences.

A	B
sore broken feel sprained high pain	chest leg wrist temperature throat sick

1 I've got a _____ _____, and I can't use my computer.

2 I've got a very _____ _____.

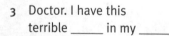

3 Doctor. I have this terrible _____ in my _____.

4 Yes, he has a _____ _____.

5 I can't eat any more. I _____ _____.

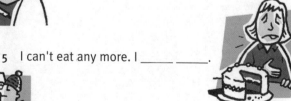

6 I went skiing, but now I've got a _____ _____.

3 Correct the mistakes in the sentences.

1 Have you got an aspirin? I feel a terrible headache.

2 I can't eat anything. I feel to be sick.

3 You don't look well. Are you a high temperature?

4 Steve is in hospital. I think he's got the broken arm.

5 I'm going to try acupuncture for my backache.

6 I don't feel very good. I've got cold.

7 I'm staying at home. I've feel the flu.

Grammar | purpose/reason/result

4 Complete the sentences with words or phrases from the box.

> to   because   that   so that I
> not to   in order   because it   so

1 Can you turn the music down so _____ I can hear the telephone?

2 They moved house _____ to be near the train station.

3 I came here _____ I want to ask your advice.

4 I am writing _____ invite you to our party.

5 She was out _____ I left her a message.

6 We have to leave very early in order _____ miss the train.

7 I cycle to school _____ don't have to sit in traffic all morning.

8 I swim every day _____ is good for my back.

5 Complete the sentences using *because, so, so that* or *to*. If *so* and *so that* are possible, use *so that*.

1 I went to the chemist _____ get some medicine.

2 Jane bought a car _____ she hated getting the bus to work.

3 I stopped eating biscuits _____ I can lose weight.

4 We arrived early _____ buy the tickets.

5 He was angry _____ his train was late.

6 I didn't know the answer _____ I asked Jack.

7 They wanted Lisa to come to the party _____ she could meet Tim.

8 I get up early _____ I can have breakfast before I leave.

9 I sent a message to Kate _____ ask for some money.

10 I work very hard _____ now I'm the manager.

Writing

6 a Match the letters (1–3) to the pictures (A–C).

Dear John,
Firstly, (1) _____ and green
vegetables in (2) _____ vitamins.
(3) _____ hot drinks for
your throat? Then you should stay at home and rest.

Dear Lucy,
You need to relax. Try
(4) _____, and
a hot bath or shower
before you go to bed. You
shouldn't drink tea or
coffee, but you could
try camomile tea*,
because it (5) _____
_____. Sweet dreams.

3

Dear Sam,
Maybe you are eating
something that your
stomach doesn't like. Go
to a specialist so (6) _____
_____
_. (7) _____
_____ to help move your
stomach muscles, and
don't eat in the evenings
before you go to bed.

---

camomile – a small yellow flower

b Use these phrases to complete the letters.

a You should try doing some exercises
b order to give you more
c you should try eating lots of fruit
d that he/she can tell you what to eat
e having a massage to help with stress
f Why don't you try making
g helps you to relax

Listening

7 a **7·2** Cover the tapescript. Listen to the interview and answer the question.

Shiatsu is

A a type of Swiss massage.
B a Japanese medicine.
C a type of Japanese massage.
D a Chinese mushroom.

b Listen again and complete the notes in the table.

SHIATSU	
What are the main beliefs?	Like (1)___ it believes that there are channels of (2)___.
Where is it from?	It is a (3)___ massage.
What happens in a typical session?	• Firstly, the practitioner will (4)___ about your health. • Then, he/she will give you a (5)___. • Lastly, he/she will (6)___ points on your body.
What does it treat?	It is very good for (7)___, stomachaches and (8)___.
How long does it take?	A session takes about (9)___.
Do patients always feel better immediately?	(10)___. Sometimes it takes (11)___ sessions.

TAPESCRIPT

Woman: So what is Shiatsu?

Man: Well, it's a type of massage. It's like acupuncture because it believes that there are channels of energy. You press on different points on the body and the energy moves around better.

Woman: I see. Where is it from?

Man: Shiatsu is a Japanese massage, but now you can have Shiatsu treatments in many countries.

Woman: Right. And what happens in a typical session?

Man: First, the Shiatsu practitioner asks you questions about your health, and your problem. Then he gives you a massage to relax the muscles. Lastly, he presses points on your body. He usually uses his hands, but sometimes he uses his arms, elbows, knees and feet.

Woman: His feet? OK. So what problems can it treat?

Man: It's very good for problems like backache, stomachache and headache, but it works for other problems too.

Woman: That's good. How long does it take?

Man: Each session usually takes about an hour.

Woman: An hour. And do patients feel better after one hour?

Man: Actually, no. Some patients will feel worse at the beginning. Sometimes they need two, three or more sessions before they feel better.

Vocabulary | speed

1 Match the sentence halves.

1 A jumbo jet
2 Snails move
3 A Mercedes has a top
4 The speed
5 The Harry Potter books are the fastest
6 Mexico City has the worst rush
7 British roads have had speed

a -selling children's books in history.
b hour in the world.
c cameras since 1992.
d speed of 180 km per hour.
e travels at 885 km per hour.
f limit in Nevada US is 55 km per hour.
g at 0.0028 m a second.

2 Complete the text using words from the box.

up   down   behind   in   on   up   with

Are you always (1) _____ a hurry? Do you often get (2) _____ with your work? Do you have to stay late in the office to catch (3) _____ _____ your work? Do you panic when you can't arrive (4) _____ time? Why? Stop worrying! The world is 25 billion years old. It will continue with or without you. You need to slow (5) _____, not speed (6) _____! Join the Slow Living movement and see a better, slower world. Join today! Or tomorrow . . . or next week . . . or . . .

Grammar | Present Simple passive

3 Complete the sentences with a verb from the box. Use the Present Simple passive.

take   stop   spend   give   write
make   play   wash

1 Our pizzas _____ with fresh ingredients.
2 This book _____ by a very famous author.
3 Football is the only sport that _____ in almost every country.
4 He _____ by customs every time he enters the country.
5 I _____ to work by taxi every morning.
6 Most of our money _____ on food and drink.
7 The dirty clothes _____ in the washing machine.
8 I _____ £20 pocket money every week by my parents.

4 Make questions using the prompts and the Present Simple passive. The answers to the quiz are below.

1 What food / Italy / know / for?
 A pizza   B hamburgers   C apples
2 What meat / not serve / to Hindus?
 A chicken   B beef   C pork
3 How much / milk / drink / in US compared to fizzy drinks?
 A 1/5   B 1/2   C 3/4
4 What complaint / hear / most often in US fast food restaurants?
 A the food is too expensive
 B there isn't enough meat in the hamburger
 C there's too much ice in the drink
5 Which animal / not eat / by Muslims?
 A cow   B sheep   C pig
6 How many teaspoons of sugar / contain / in one glass of cola?
 A 1   B 5   C 14

2B 3A 4C 5C 6C

Answers

Reading

5 **a** Read the text and answer the questions. <u>Underline</u> the best answer.

1 When did the first Pret a Manger open?
   A 1980   B 1986   C 1950

2 How is the food made?
   A in a factory
   B by chefs in the sandwich shops every day
   C by chefs the night before

3 What does Pret a Manger sell?
   A only sandwiches
   B only sandwiches and sushi
   C sandwiches, sushi and other types of food

4 How can you find information about the calories in each dish?
   A look on the website
   B ask the Pret a Manger workers
   C write to Mr Metcalfe or Mr Beecham

5 What happens to the food that isn't eaten?
   A They throw it away.
   B It is recycled.
   C Charities take it.

★ PRET A MANGER ★

In the 1980s Julian Metcalfe and Sinclair Beecham spent a lot of time walking around London looking for a good, fast lunch. They never found one. So in 1986 they opened their own sandwich shop, Pret a Manger. Today there are 150 Pret a Mangers in the UK and Hong Kong. Why has Pret a Manger become successful? Firstly, the food. Every night a van delivers fresh ingredients to the Pret a Manger stores. Early in the morning the chefs check the ingredients carefully, and then they make fresh sandwiches for the day. And these days it isn't only sandwiches. Pret a Manger sells many different types of food: it even includes sushi on the menu. Quality and care is important for the company. For people who want to know exactly what they are eating, Pret a Manger's website gives information about each dish. For example, if you want to know how many calories are in a ham and cheese sandwich, you can find out. Pret a Manger also does good things for the community. At the end of the day, charities take any extra unwanted food and give it to homeless people.
McDonald's owns 33% of the company, and this is one reason why people all over the world now know the name, Pret a Manger.

b Complete the sentences. Decide if the sentences are active or passive.

1 Every night fresh ingredients _____ to the Pret a Manger stores. (deliver)

2 The ingredients _____ early in the morning. (check)

3 Fresh sandwiches _____ every day. (make)

4 Pret a Manger _____ many different types of food. (serve)

5 Pret a Manger's website _____ information about each dish. (give)

6 Unwanted food _____ to charities. (give)

7 33% of the company _____ by McDonald's. (own)

8 Pret a Manger _____ by people all over the world. (know)

How to ...

6 **a** Match the sentence halves.

1 The economies of the poorer countries
2 Violent crime
3 Air pollution is getting
4 The team's results are
5 Oil prices have gone
6 The cost of housing has

a worse.
b fallen steadily in the last three years.
c has risen slightly in the last five years.
d have got better in the last twenty years.
e improving steadily.
f up dramatically this year.

b Match the sentences in Ex. 6a to the diagrams below.

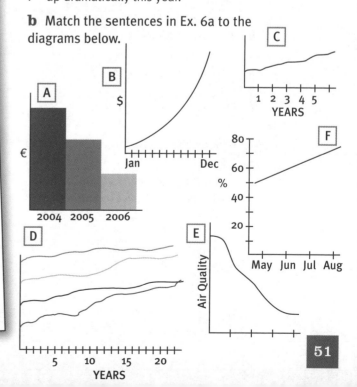

Vocabulary | phrasal verbs

1 Complete the gaps in the text with a verb from A and a preposition from B. Put the verbs in the correct form.

A	B
split	out
get	out with
go	apart
put	up with
ask	up
grow	over

Milly and Ahmed met in a bar. She ¹ _____ him _____ and they went to the cinema the next day. After that they started ² _____ _____ _____ each other, but things didn't go well. He was only interested in gardening and she was only interested in business, and soon they started to ³ _____ _____. She was always working late and never had time to see him. He couldn't ⁴ _____ _____ _____ it, so finally they ⁵ _____ _____. But he soon ⁶ _____ _____ it, and they stayed friends. Later she became a rich businesswoman and employed him as her gardener.

2 Underline the correct sentence.

1. a I split up with him.
   b I split up him.
   c I split with him up.

2. a I asked out her and she said yes.
   b I asked out and she said yes.
   c I asked her out and she said yes.

3. a We grew us apart.
   b We grew apart us.
   c We grew apart.

4. a I'm going with a nice man out.
   b I'm going out with a nice man.
   c I'm going nice man out with.

5. a I over got him.
   b I got over him.
   c I got him over.

6. a I hate that dog. I can't put up with.
   b I hate that dog. I can't put up with it.
   c I hate that dog. I can't put it up with.

Grammar | questions

3 Six of the questions have a mistake. Find the mistakes and correct them.

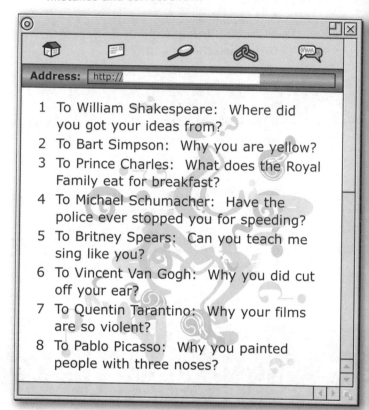

Address: http://

1 To William Shakespeare: Where did you got your ideas from?
2 To Bart Simpson: Why you are yellow?
3 To Prince Charles: What does the Royal Family eat for breakfast?
4 To Michael Schumacher: Have the police ever stopped you for speeding?
5 To Britney Spears: Can you teach me sing like you?
6 To Vincent Van Gogh: Why you did cut off your ear?
7 To Quentin Tarantino: Why your films are so violent?
8 To Pablo Picasso: Why you painted people with three noses?

4 **a** Match 1–8 to a–h to make questions.

1	Who's your	a	been on TV?
2	Do you	b	do in your free time?
3	What do you	c	when you were a child?
4	Did you go to	d	dream holiday?
5	Do you think	e	you are a happy person?
6	Have you ever	f	like sport?
7	Were you shy	g	favourite film star?
8	What is your	h	bed late last night?

b Match the questions in Ex. 4a to the answers.

Answers

A A month in the desert with a camel. = Question ___

B A little bit, but I'm not now. = Question ___

C About 12.00. = Question ___

D Not really, but I sometimes go skiing. = Question ___

E Sean Connery. = Question ___

F Yes. I'm always laughing. = Question ___

G I like learning languages and travelling. = Question ___

H Not yet. = Question ___

5 Make questions for the answers.

1 _____ _____ you from?
I'm from Germany.

2 What _____ _____ job?
I am a writer.

3 _____ _____ you study?
I studied German literature.

4 _____ _____ your hobbies?
My hobbies are swimming and playing the piano.

5 How _____ brothers and sisters _____ _____ have?
I have two brothers and one sister.

6 _____ _____ done speed-dating before?
No, I haven't.

7 _____ are you _____ back to Germany?
I'm going back to Germany in August.

8 _____ _____ come back to England?
Yes, I will.

9 _____ _____ you think of speed-dating?
I think it's strange but good fun.

10 What _____ _____ reading at the moment?
I'm reading *How to Find your Perfect Partner*.

Listening

6 **a** **8.1** Cover the tapescript. Listen to a US immigration officer interviewing a man. Tick (✓) the things they talk about.

jobs ☐   education ☐
the weather ☐   clothes ☐
children ☐   hobbies ☐
family ☐

b Listen again and complete the notes.

NOTES
Mr Marius Cecillon   Miss Judith Stein
Job: translator   Job: works in a _____

Met in _____, _____ years ago.

Miss Stein studied _____ at New Mexico State University.
Hobbies: goes to _____ in the _____ 3 or 4 times a week.

TAPESCRIPT

IO: So, Mr Cecillon, we're going to ask you a few questions, OK?

C: OK.

IO: What's your job?

C: I'm a translator.

IO: How long have you been a translator?

C: About ten years, more or less.

IO: What languages?

C: English into French.

IO: Uh huh. OK. Now I'm going to ask you about your relationship with Miss Stein.

C: OK.

IO: Where did you meet?

C: We met in Paris, in France.

IO: When was this?

C: It was four years ago.

IO: Four years ago. And what does she do?

C: She works in a bank.

IO: Have you met her family, Mr Cecillon?

C: Her family? No. Well, I just met her brother once.

IO: OK. Miss Stein went to university, didn't she?

C: Yes.

IO: Do you know where? Which university?

C: Yes, she was at NMSU, New Mexico State University.

IO: Uh huh. And what did she study?

C: She studied Economics.

IO: Sorry?

C: She studied Economics.

IO: OK. Does Miss Stein have any hobbies?

C: She goes to the gym.

IO: Does she go often?

C: She goes three or four times a week.

IO: When? What time of day?

C: Well, she usually goes in the evening.

IO: Do you go with her?

C: No, I'm not very sporty.

IO: Too busy translating, I guess.

C: Yeah.

Grammar | Past Continuous and Past Simple

1 Choose the correct alternative.

1 I *was watching/watched* TV when the lights *were going/went* out.

2 She *was getting up/got up* and *was having/had* a shower.

3 *Weren't you meeting/Didn't you meet* him when you *were being/were* at university?

4 We *were driving/drove* across France when the car *was breaking down/broke down*.

5 I *was finding/found* $10 while I *was walking/walked* home yesterday.

6 He *was losing/lost* his wallet when he *was playing/played* with the children.

2 Complete the sentences using the verbs in brackets in the Past Simple or Past Continuous.

Where were you when...?

Dionne Grobler

I (1) _____ (watch) TV when I (2) _____ (hear) about the astronauts landing on the Moon. It (3) _____ (be) an amazing moment for the whole world. In those days many people (4) _____ (not have) a TV. I (5) _____ (call) my neighbours on the phone and they said they (6) _____ (listen) to it on the radio so I (7) _____ (invite) them to my house and we watched it on TV together.

Marsha Vygotsky

I heard the news when I (8) _____ (sit) at the table eating my breakfast. I (9) _____ (be) a musician then, in a band. The Beatles (10) _____ (not be) our heroes, but we loved John Lennon. We heard the newsreader say, 'John Lennon was killed while he (11) _____ (walk) home in New York,' and we just (12) _____ (not know) what to say.

Billy Fingleman

I (13) _____ (study) for my Masters in Politics at the time. In fact, I (14) _____ (read) a book in the university library when I (15) _____ (hear) all this noise outside. Someone said the Berlin Wall was coming down and we all (16) _____ (go) to the square and celebrated. The party (17) _____ (not finish) until 6.00 a.m.

Pronunciation

3 **a** **8.2** Cover the tapescript. Listen and complete the sentences.

1 _____ it raining? _____, it _____.

2 _____ you dreaming? _____, I _____.

3 _____ she smoking? _____, she _____.

4 _____ they playing? _____, they _____.

5 _____ you running? _____, we _____.

6 _____ he singing? _____, he _____.

b Listen again and mark the stress. Check your answers with the tapescript.

> **TAPESCRIPT**
>
> 1 Was it <u>rain</u>ing? <u>No</u>, it <u>was</u>n't.
> 2 Were you <u>dream</u>ing? <u>Yes</u>, I <u>was</u>.
> 3 Was she <u>smok</u>ing? <u>Yes</u>, she <u>was</u>.
> 4 Were they <u>play</u>ing? <u>No</u> they <u>weren't</u>.
> 5 Were you <u>run</u>ning? <u>Yes</u>, we <u>were</u>.
> 6 Was he <u>sing</u>ing? <u>No</u>, he <u>wasn't</u>.

Writing

4 **a** Choose the best alternative.

1 A strange thing happened (last summer)/summer last. [1]

2 *After a while/While after* the noise got louder, . . . [ ]

3 *In end/In the end* I realised the noise had been my cat fighting this bird! [ ]

4 *Beginning,/To begin with*, I thought it was the wind, but . . . [ ]

5 *So I decided/So I did decide* to see what it was. [ ]

6 *One night/Late night* I was lying in bed when I heard a noise on the roof. [ ]

7 I climbed onto the roof and *a sudden/suddenly* a bird flew past my face! [ ]

b Put the sentences in order to make the story. Write the numbers in the boxes.

Reading

5　**a**　Read the text, then look at sentences 1–6. Did these things happen? Write Y (yes), N (no), or DK (don't know).

1　Betty's teacher saw her running.
2　Betty's home town gave her a present after she won the Olympic gold.
3　Betty's cousin died in the plane crash.
4　Betty broke her leg.
5　Betty won gold in the 1932 Olympics.
6　Betty continued running for the rest of her life.

SPEEDY BETTY
The Incredible Story Of An Olympic Champion

One day in the 1920s, a Biology teacher was sitting in a train when he saw one of his students. This student, a teenager called Betty Robinson, was running to catch the train. The teacher was <u>amazed</u>. She was the fastest girl he had ever seen.

With her teacher's help, Betty started <u>training</u>. Less than two years later she was an Olympic champion. Betty won the 100 metres at the Amsterdam Olympics in 1928. She was sixteen years old, and it was only her fourth race. When she arrived home the US was in love with her. Big <u>crowds</u> shouted her name in the streets. Her home town gave her a diamond watch and her school gave her a silver cup.

But then disaster. Three years after the Olympics, Betty and her cousin were involved in a plane crash. Betty was <u>unconscious</u> for seven weeks and her leg was badly broken. Doctors thought she would die. But she <u>recovered</u> slowly. It took her two years to learn how to walk again.

She missed the 1932 Olympics, but she returned to the American team in 1936, where again she won a gold medal, this time in the 100 metres relay. Betty was involved in athletics for the rest of her life. She died in 1999, aged 87, a true sporting hero.

b　Number the events in order.

☐ **A**　Betty won her second gold medal.
☐ **B**　Betty won the 100 metres at the Amsterdam Olympics.
☐ **C**　Betty received a diamond watch.
☐ **D**　A teacher saw Betty running to catch a train.
☐ **E**　Betty's plane crashed.
☐ **F**　Betty spent two years learning to walk again.

c　Match the underlined words in the text to these definitions.

1　got better after an illness or problem
2　learn the skills for a job or activity
3　lots of people in one place
4　very surprised
5　not awake

Vocabulary | jobs

1 Match the jobs to the pictures.

1 plumber ___   5 firefighter ___
2 mechanic ___   6 nurse ___
3 lawyer ___   7 factory worker ___
4 accountant ___ 8 sales rep ___

2 Match the sentence halves.

1 One day I would like to run
2 Before I can get a new job, I need to prepare
3 He didn't like the job so he
4 If I do this job well, I might
5 As a doctor, I have to work
6 My sister had an interview
7 I have applied for a job
8 His interview went well and he was
9 Are you going to take

a long hours.
b get promoted.
c as Managing Director.
d offered the job.
e my own company.
f the job?
g resigned.
h my CV.
i for the job yesterday.

3 Choose the correct words to complete the texts.

A Agnieska had lots of (1) _____ from university, but she worked as an (2) _____ in a chocolate (3) _____. She was reliable and worked long hours. She was never sick. Her employer noticed her hard work and gave her a (4) _____ at the end of the year. After five years with the (5) _____, she became the Managing Director.

B Mirko prepared his (6) _____ and filled in the application form. He was applying for a job as sales rep for a computer software (7) _____. He didn't have any (8) _____, but he had some work (9) _____ selling mobile phones. When he went for the interview, he was asked to wait in the office. After three and a half hours, the (10) _____ still hadn't arrived. Mirko went home.

1 A interviewees B qualifcations C employers
2 A employee B application C experience
3 A bonus B factory C Director
4 A salary B qualification C bonus
5 A company B experience C employee
6 A salary B CV C experience
7 A bonus B Director C company
8 A qualifications B experience C salary
9 A employer B interviewer C experience
10 A interviewer B sales rep C company

Pronunciation

4 **a** **9.1** Listen and complete the sentences.

1 Do you have any _____?
2 Have you filled in an _____ _____?
3 I've got five years _____.
4 What _____ do you offer?
5 I'm an _____.
6 Ask the _____.
7 He's the _____ _____.
8 She works in a _____.
9 He runs his own _____.
10 Have you sent your _____?

b Listen again. Mark the main stress on the words you wrote.

Listening

5 **a** Read the sentences. Mark them GI (good idea) or BI (bad idea).

When you write your CV

1 write a minimum of three pages.
2 check your spelling.

3 use a computer.
4 say you have lots of qualifications, even if you do not have them.
5 give information about your junior school and all your hobbies.

b **9.2** Listen and check your answers.

6 Choose the correct alternative.

1 5% of the CVs that Melanie reads are *good/ bad/OK*.
2 She thinks a CV should be *more than two pages long/exactly two pages long/two pages long or less*.
3 25% of CVs she receives contain *lies/true information/love letters*.
4 Melanie says that people lie about *their hobbies/qualifications/contact details*.
5 You should *write a new CV for each job/use the same CV for every job/write a new CV every month*.
6 A Danish woman sent some Danish *perfume/ clothes/food* with her CV.
7 She *was given the job/wasn't given the job/ became a chef*.

TAPESCRIPT

M: I read hundreds of CVs every week. Most of them are good. A few are excellent. And about five per cent of them are terrible.

I: Really? What makes a bad CV?

M: There are a number of things. A CV should be short. No more than two pages long. I recently read a CV that was twenty pages long.

I: Unbelievable.

M: But usually the problems are quite simple.

I: What type of things?

M: Spelling mistakes. People who write their CV with a pen, not on computer. But the worst thing is that twenty-five per cent of CVs are not true.

I: What do you mean?

M: People tell lies. They say they have certain qualifications and we find that they don't have them.

I: So what advice can you give about writing a CV?

M: Read the advert carefully. Learn as much as possible about the job. Then write a new CV specially for this job. Write it on a computer and only write what is important for this job.

I: Are there any imaginative or interesting ideas that work?

M: There was a woman from Denmark who applied for a job in an office. She sent some Danish food with her CV to remind us that she was from Denmark. And she got the job.

Vocabulary | *make* and *do*

1 There are mistakes in six of the sentences. Find the mistakes and correct them.

1 He sits in his office all day making absolutely nothing.
2 Have you done a decision about where to go on holiday?
3 She makes an effort to be friendly to all her employees.
4 Can you make me a favour?
5 I have made a lot of research on the Internet.
6 Good luck in the interview. You can only do your best.
7 Have you done an appointment to see the doctor?
8 The food was cold so we did a complaint.

2 Complete the sentences using expressions with *make* or *do*, and the words in brackets.

1 She's getting better at Maths. I really think she's _____. (progress)
2 They _____ _____ _____ into why the weather is changing. (research)
3 We have got a History lesson today. Have you _____ your _____? (homework)
4 I often travel to Asia because my company _____ a lot of _____ in China. (business)
5 She isn't very good at _____ _____. (decisions)
6 He isn't working very hard. He should _____ an _____. (effort)
7 When the computer arrived it was broken, so we _____ a _____. (complaint)
8 I don't know what he does but I think he _____ a lot of _____. (money)

Grammar: *can/could/be able to*

3 Complete the sentences using *can*, *can't*, *could* or *couldn't* and verbs from the box.

> speak understand take cook sleep
> finish believe hear catch sing

1 My grandmother was a linguist. She _____ _____ six languages fluently.
2 I _____ _____ why they haven't phoned us yet.
3 They took us to the station so we _____ _____ the train to Manchester.
4 I feel so tired because I _____ _____ last night.
5 I can play the guitar but I _____ _____. My voice is terrible.
6 That's impossible! I _____ _____ that what you are telling me is true.
7 I've brought my camera with me, so I _____ _____ some photos.
8 When I turned the music off, I _____ _____ someone knocking at the door.
9 Tim is very fast at doing crosswords. Usually, he _____ _____ one in just three minutes.
10 My mother always cooked for me, so I _____ even _____ a plate of spaghetti when I left home.

4 Complete the sentences using *can*, *can't*, *could*, *couldn't* or *be able to*.

1 Can you speak up a little? I _____ hear you.
2 Samantha _____ paint beautiful landscapes, but she can't paint people.
3 I want to _____ speak English fluently.
4 I _____ ski when I was younger, but now I'm not good at it.
5 She's been on a diet and now she _____ wear a size 8!
6 I'm sorry, but we won't _____ come to the wedding because we are on holiday then.
7 I _____ walk in these shoes. They're too big.
8 He _____ understand why everyone was laughing. Then he saw his photo.
9 _____ you come to the party tomorrow? I need to tell Marta.
10 I _____ do Maths at school, and I'm still not good at numbers.

Reading

5 Read the text and write notes in the table below.

Abigail Sin, 10 – Singapore
Abigail Sin could read when she was two, started playing the piano at five and now, at age ten, she can play so well that she plays as a professional pianist in the Singapore Concert Hall. Her twin brother, Josiah, who doesn't like music, says he can't understand why she practises so much. 'She plays the same things again and again.'

Ali Fukuhara, 14 – Japan
Then there is the Japanese 'Tiger Woods of table tennis', Ali Fukuhara, who started to play ping-pong when she was just three years old. She was so small that she couldn't see over the table. Two years later she could beat opponents who were three years older than her, and now she is training for the Olympics. She used to cry when she lost a game, but now she says she can control that.

Nguyen Ngod Truong Son, 12 – Vietnam
At three years old, Nguyen used to watch his mother and father play chess. He always asked them if he could play too. Eventually, they let him play and he showed them that he knew how to move the pieces already. One month later he could beat his parents. When he was seven, he played in national tournaments, and won. His father says, 'He was born with a natural gift.' He hopes that soon Nguyen will be able to beat the grand masters of chess, and he probably will!

	Special talent	When did he/ she start?	Achievements or hopes for the future
Abigail Sin			
Ali Fukuhara			
Nguyen Ngod Truong Son			

Pronunciation

6 a [9.3] Listen to the pronunciation of *can*, *can't*, *could* or *couldn't* in the sentences. Are these words stressed (S) or unstressed (U)?

1 She can play the piano.
2 She can win the Olympics.
3 He can't understand.
4 You can't teach a baby to play chess.
5 He could write his own music when he was four.
6 She could read when she was two.
7 She couldn't see over the table.
8 They couldn't believe what they saw.

b Practise saying the sentences.

Lifelong learning

7 a [9.4] Cover the tapescript. Listen and complete the notes with the activities a–f..

Setting targets – my Spanish

I can ^{1} ...
     ^{2} ...
I can't ^{3} ...
I want to be able to ^{4} ...
I am going to ^{5} ...
              ^{6} ...

a talk more fluently.
b write down new words in a book.
c speak to Angela in Spanish every week.
d read texts quite well, but I need a dictionary.
e ask questions if I don't understand.
f remember the vocabulary we learn in class.

b Complete the notes for you.

TAPESCRIPT
I think my Spanish is getting better, especially my reading. I can read the texts in the book now, and I understand them quite well. Sometimes I need to look up words in a dictionary or ask my teacher. She's taught us some phrases to use if we don't understand, so that's OK.

One problem I have is that I don't remember new words, the new vocabulary that we learn in the lessons. I'm going to write down all the new words in a small book, so that I can learn them. I want to be able to talk more fluently, but I can't remember the words, so it is very difficult. I'm also going to practise speaking in Spanish with Angela, my classmate. We're going to meet before the lesson every week, and spend half an hour talking in Spanish. I think that will really help me too.

Vocabulary | crime

1 Use words from the box to describe what happened in the pictures. You may need to change the verb forms.

> judge thief jury police officer steal
> arrest innocent punishment fine prison sentence

1 The _____ gave the criminal a 5-year _____.

2 The _____ _____ a bicycle and had to pay a £100 _____ as his _____.

3 The _____ _____ a young woman.

4 The _____ decided that the woman was _____.

2 a Complete the table using the words from the box.

> mugging shoplifter murder thief pickpocket
> burglar rob

CRIME	CRIMINAL	VERB
theft	(a) robber/_____	to steal something
robbery	robber	to (b) _____ (a bank/someone)
burglary	(c) _____	to burgle a house
(d) _____	mugger	to mug someone
pick pocketing	(e) _____	to pick someone's pocket
shoplifting	(f) _____	to shoplift
(g) _____	murderer	to murder someone

b Match the verbs in Ex. 2a to the definitions.

1 to take something from a shop without paying for it _____
2 to take illegally from a house _____
3 to take someone's money/wallet from their bag/pocket, without the person noticing _____
4 to take something that is not yours _____
5 to kill someone _____
6 to attack and take something from someone (on the street) _____
7 to steal money or items from a bank or shop _____

Grammar | Past Simple passive

3 Underline the correct form of the verb.

1 The old lady *was mugged/mug* in the street yesterday.
2 The murderer *arrested/was arrested*.
3 The shoplifter *was given/gave* a fine.
4 My wallet *was taken/took* by a pickpocket.
5 The bank *rob/was robbed*. They *took/was taken* £10,000.
6 The jury *decided/was decided* that he was guilty.
7 My computer *stole/was stolen* from the library.
8 My house *was burgled/burgled* last week.
9 The burglars *stole/were stolen* the DVD player.
10 The politician *was punished/punished* for not paying his taxes.

4 Use the Past Simple active or passive to complete the sentences.

1 I _____ (ask) to give a presentation about my work.
2 Jo _____ (buy) some new CDs with the money he _____ (give) for his birthday.
3 I _____ (leave) my purse in the restaurant and it _____ (steal).
4 The two men _____ (take) our suitcases from the car.
5 They _____ (tell) the concert _____ (start) at 7.30 p.m.
6 _____ you _____ (invite) to the wedding?
7 He _____ (meet) at the station by a taxi driver.
8 The car _____ (drive) by a man wearing a black hat.

5 Make questions using the Past Simple active or passive.

POLICE REPORT: EGYPTIAN VASE
STOLEN: 1 _____ , 2004
TIME: 2 _____ p.m.
PLACE: 3 _____ Museum
REPORTED BY: 4 _____

5 €_____ REWARD OFFERED

FOUND: IN AN 6 _____ SHOP
(BY MRS G)
RETURNED TO POLICE BY MRS G
DATE: 7 _____ SEPT, 2004

1 When was the *vase stolen?*
2 What time _____?
3 Where _____?
4 Who _____?
5 How much _____?
6 Where _____?
7 When was _____?

Reading

6 Read the text and answer the questions.

1 What was David Morris trying to steal?
2 Where did he go?
3 How many times did he try?
4 Was he successful?
5 Where did the lady in the chemist put his note?
6 Where did he go next?
7 Why didn't the owner of the Italian shop read the note?
8 Why did the manager of the restaurant go into the back room?
9 Who telephoned the police?
10 What did the police do?

Writing

7 **a** Label the paragraphs in Ex. 6: *Introduction*, *Story* or *Conclusion*.

b Put the sentences below in order, to make a story.

Better luck next time

David Morris was an unsuccessful robber. He walked into a shop with a note which read, 'I have a gun in my pocket. I will shoot you if you don't give me the money.'

First, he went into a chemist. The female assistant took the note but she didn't read it, she just threw it in the bin. The thief left the shop with nothing. He tried the Italian shop next door. The owner of the shop took the note and looked at it. He shook his head. 'I'm sorry, sir,' he replied, 'but I can't read English.'

The man tried one last time. He went to a Chinese takeaway restaurant. The manager there took the note, said that he didn't have his glasses and he had to go into the back room to find them. While he was there, he telephoned the police, who arrived shortly afterwards and arrested the failed robber.

One-legged thief is caught

During the fight, Ghansyam pulled off Eric's false leg by mistake, but then the thief escaped by hopping into his car.

A shopkeeper helped to catch a burglar who only had one leg.

Mr Patel said, 'It was a real shock when his leg came off in my hands.'

Ghansyam Patel, who is 56, fought with Eric Gardener, after Eric tried to rob him in the street.

However, later he tried to order a new leg, and the police arrested him. Gardener, 41, was jailed for three years after he said he was guilty.

First conditional

1 Put the verb in brackets into the correct form.

1 If you go running everyday, you _____ better. (feel)

2 I'll come out later if I _____ this report. (finish)

3 If it _____ raining, shall we go for a walk? (stop)

4 If she _____ her exams, we'll buy her a new CD player. (pass)

5 You _____ late if you don't hurry up. (be)

6 If we _____ time to visit her, we'll phone instead. (not have)

7 Will you visit the British Museum if you _____ to London? (go)

8 If I _____ asleep now, I'll be tired tomorrow. (not fall)

9 We might go and see a film later if Pete _____ to come. (want)

10 If the course starts tomorrow, _____ you _____ to the first lesson? (come)

Gerunds vs infinitives

2 Complete the sentences with the verbs in brackets.

1 I miss _____ (go) to the beach at the weekends.

2 I didn't expect _____ (see) you here this morning.

3 We decided _____ (change) the date of the meeting.

4 Will you consider _____ (move) to America?

5 They have offered _____ (help) me find a flat.

6 Will you promise _____ (write) to me every day?

7 I don't want _____ (see) her again.

8 She didn't enjoy _____ (meet) all the managers.

9 He seems _____ (be) happy in his new job.

10 We can't afford _____ (buy) a house in the centre.

Present Simple passive

3 Complete the sentences using the Present Simple passive of the verbs in the box.

> clean   build   send   deliver   employ
> close   recycle   do   make   not use

1 The newspapers _____ on Sundays.

2 The office _____ every morning.

3 These houses _____ in just three weeks.

4 He _____ by a big computer company.

5 This car _____ very much now, so we're going to sell it.

6 Most children's toys _____ in China.

7 The bottles _____ to help the environment.

8 The letters _____ at the end of the week.

9 The work _____ by professionals.

10 The school _____ during the summer.

Past Continuous vs Past Simple

4 Underline the correct verb form.

1 It *was raining /rained* when the accident *was happening /happened*.

2 When I *was coming /came* in everyone *was talking /talked* about me.

3 We *were having /had* a coffee when the stranger *asked /was asking* for Louise's number.

4 I *was travelling /travelled* in Asia when I *heard /was hearing* the news.

5 It *was /was being* a beautiful morning. The sun *was shining /shone* and the birds *were singing /sang*.

6 I *was walking /walked* through the park when I *met /was meeting* an old friend.

7 Mike *was listening /listened* to music so he *didn't hear /wasn't hearing* the telephone.

8 I *was going /went* to work when I *remembered /was remembering* I didn't have my keys.

9 As soon as I *got /was getting* home I *went / was going* to bed.

10 I *was watching /watched* television at 2 a.m. this morning.

can/could/be able to

5 Complete the sentences using *can/can't/could /couldn't/be able to*.

1 I'm very busy next week, so I won't _____ meet you.

2 I _____ open this door. Can you help me?

3 When I was in Kiev I _____ understand what anyone was saying.

4 She's very good at languages. When she was eight, she _____ read Greek and Latin.

5 I'm sorry, but Mr Harding _____ see you today. He's out of the office.

6 I _____ get tickets for the concert. They were sold out.

7 When I finish this course, I'll _____ to speak Japanese fluently.

8 When I was a student, I _____ afford to eat out because I was poor.

9 I'm frightened of water because I _____ swim.

10 _____ you come for a drink later?

Past Simple passive

6 Rewrite the sentences in the Past Simple passive. Start with the words given.

1 Someone took my bag.
My ...

2 They arrested the thief outside the bank.
The thief ...

3 People built the museum in 2001.
The museum ...

4 They met the President at the airport.
The President ...

5 Someone checked all their passports carefully.
All their ...

6 Someone told them about the delays.
They ...

7 Someone finished all the work over the weekend.
All the work ...

8 Someone invited the employees to a party.
The employees ...

9 Someone asked him to work seven days a week.
He ...

10 Someone damaged the piano when they carried it upstairs.
The piano ...

Vocabulary

7 Complete the sentences with a word from the box.

> ill hard-working flu hurry sore
> chatty handsome broken toe skinny

1 I need to see a doctor about my _____ throat.

2 She doesn't eat very much and that's why she's so _____.

3 I love Tom Hanks. He's so _____.

4 She never leaves work before 9 p.m. She is so _____.

5 Ouch! I just banged my _____ on the door.

6 I feel terrible. I think I've got _____.

7 I fell down the stairs, and now I've got a _____ arm.

8 I feel _____. I hope it isn't food poisoning.

9 We spend a long time on the telephone because Meera is so _____.

10 Can you drive a bit faster because I'm in a _____?

8 Complete the sentences using verbs from the box. You may have to change the verb form.

> run arrive do deteriorate have
> ask apply make work catch

1 He enjoys his new job but he has to _____ very long hours.

2 If we don't send the letter today, it won't _____ on time.

3 Shaun _____ Joanne out on a date.

4 The quality of the material we use has _____.

5 I missed last week's lessons, so I need to _____ up with the grammar.

6 I'm very ambitious, so I would like to _____ my own company.

7 He _____ for a job as an air steward.

8 Don't worry about your exams. Just _____ your best.

9 I study hard but I'm not _____ very much progress.

10 Yesterday, I _____ an interview for a job as manager.

10.1 Wildlife

Vocabulary | animals

1 Find fourteen animals in the word square. All the words go from left to right.

t	i	g	e	r	w	o	l	f
e	l	e	p	h	a	n	t	j
h	i	g	e	a	g	l	e	h
s	k	i	c	o	w	c	a	t
s	n	t	s	p	i	d	e	r
d	o	g	f	s	n	a	k	e
b	e	a	r	z	e	b	r	a
h	o	r	s	e	g	r	d	s
h	y	e	n	a	l	i	o	n

2 Complete the sentences with an animal idiom. Use a word from the boxes in each gap

> more   as   sea   the   as   mouse
> plenty   quiet   fish   in   a

He isn't really sad. He's crying *crocodile tears*.

1 Some babies make lots of noise, but he's
  _____ _____ _____ _____ _____.

2 She split up with her boyfriend, but it doesn't matter. There are _____ _____ _____ _____
  _____.

> have   eats   a   the   horse
> kittens   like   race   rat

3 That boy has had four plates of pasta. He
  _____ _____ _____ _____.

4 I hate living in a big city because I can't stand
  _____ _____ _____.

5 The kitchen looks terrible. If my mum sees it, she'll _____ _____.

> birds   the   two   bag   of   with
> cat   one   stone   let   kill   out   the

6 This is a secret, so please don't _____ _____
  _____ _____ _____ _____ _____.

7 Let's eat here and check our emails at the same time. We can _____ _____ _____
  _____ _____ _____.

Vocabulary | phrasal verbs

3 Match the <u>underlined</u> words to the phrasal verbs (a–h) with a similar meaning.

1 I <u>learned</u> Spanish <u>without trying</u>.
2 I <u>have a good relationship</u> with my sister.
3 She <u>found</u> some old photos <u>by chance</u>.
4 I <u>respect</u> my professor. He's very intelligent.
5 He <u>liked</u> London <u>immediately</u>, the first time he went there.
6 She sometimes <u>takes care of</u> her friend's baby.
7 He <u>became an adult</u> very quickly.
8 I <u>raised and educated</u> my children at home in the countryside.

a look up to _____   e get on _____
b pick up __1__   f take to _____
c bring up _____   g grow up _____
d look after _____   h come across _____

4 Complete the text using the phrasal verbs from Ex. 3. Change the verb form where necessary.

The Jungle Book

Rudyard Kipling wrote *The Jungle Book* in 1894. It tells the story of a boy called Mowgli. After his parents are killed, Mowgli is *brought up* by wolves. He (1)_____ _____ in the jungle. Mowgli is popular and he (2) _____ _____ with all the animals except Shere Khan, the tiger who killed his parents. He especially likes the panther, Bagheera, and (3)_____ _____ _____ him because Bagheera is so intelligent. One day, the wolves hear that Shere Khan is coming. They send Mowgli out of the jungle to live with people. When Mowgli goes on his journey, he (4)_____ _____ many other animals, by chance, who (5)_____ _____ him, giving him food and drink. One of these animals is Baloo, the lazy bear. Mowgli arrives and meets people, but he doesn't (6)_____ _____ life in the city, preferring the natural life of the jungle.

Penguin Popular Classics
THE JUNGLE BOOKS
RUDYARD KIPLING

5 Complete the questions using the phrasal verbs from Ex. 3. Write one word in each space.

1 A: Have _____ _____ _____ the language easily?

B: Yes, I've learned a lot of new vocabulary.

2 A: Did you _____ _____ _____ Holland?

B: Yes, I was born there and lived there for twenty years.

3 A: Have _____ ever _____ _____ any money in the street

B: Yes, I found £10 last week.

4 A: Do you _____ _____ _____ your colleagues?

B: Yes, we have a good time together.

5 A: Did _____ _____ _____ the new teacher?

B: No, I didn't like her very much.

6 A: Are you _____ _____ _____ grandmother?

B: Yes, she lives with me and I cook and clean for her.

7 A: Did you use to _____ _____ _____ your teacher?

B: Yes, everyone respected him. He knew a lot about his subject.

8 A: Were you _____ _____ _____ France?

B: Yes, I lived in France for my first fifteen years.

Pronunciation

6 a [10.1] Listen and <u>underline</u> two stressed words in each sentence.

1 I grew up in Bath.

2 I brought her up.

3 I'll look after you.

4 I look up to my mum.

5 I came across it.

6 I picked it up.

b Listen and repeat. Pay attention to the stress.

Lifelong learning

7 Look at the student's notebook. Write the corresponding number next to each strategy the student uses.

- write a definition ☐
- organise new words by topic [1]
- write example sentences ☐
- write if there is an object with new verbs ☐
- write a translation ☐

phrasal verbs - (1) Family and friends
get on (with + (2) object) -
(3) have a good relationship -
(4) s'entendre bien avec quelqu'un
(5) I get on with the other students.
I don't get on with Marek, my neighbour.

come across

How to ...

8 a Put the letters in order to make conversational phrases.

1 lelw

2 os, nayyaw

3 I aemn

4 oyu ese

b [10.2] Listen or read. What do you think the speakers say next?

1 My friend is really rich. Really, really rich. He makes millions every year. I mean he's got . . .

2 I was crying. I didn't want to get on the aeroplane. You see . . .

3 We were on the mountain. Lost. We had no food, no water and no communication. I think it was a Monday or a Tuesday. So, anyway, . . .

4 Then he asked me to marry him. A 65-year-old man! Well, . . .

c Match the endings a–d to the sentences in Ex. 8b.

a I'm scared of flying.

b I climbed down and finally saw some people.

c I said no. I was only 22. Much too young for him.

d five houses, eight cars and two boats.

Grammar | countable and uncountable nouns

1 Are the underlined words countable (C) or uncountable (U)? Write C or U.

1 Did you find much information? __
2 She went to buy a newspaper. __
3 I don't have much money. __
4 He wants some advice about his career. __
5 I've done many different jobs. __
6 We're going to do a little work, then we'll meet you later. __
7 I had a bit of good news: I passed my exam. __
8 This flat needs some new furniture. __

2 Complete the dialogues with words from the boxes.

> a few   much   quite a lot   not much

A: How (1) _____ water did you drink after the game?
B: (2) _____. I was really thirsty. And you?
A: (3) _____ because the bottle was almost empty!
B: Sorry! (4) _____ of us nearly finished the water.

> a lot   much   many   a few

A: Did you see (5) _____ animals on the safari?
B: We saw (6) _____ lions. Three or four.
A: What about elephants?
B: I've heard there are (7) _____ in the area, more than 50. But there wasn't (8) _____ time to look for them.

> none   a few   much   a lot)

A: I didn't find (9) _____ information in the library.
B: There are (10) _____ of websites with information.
A: But only (11) _____ of them are good.
B: That's true. And (12) _____ of them are free!

3 Which alternative is not possible? Cross it out.

1 I did *a lot of/some/many* work today.
2 I haven't got *much/many/any* money.
3 Can you give me *a few/some/a little bit* of advice?
4 I found *some/a lot of/a bit* information on the Internet.

5 There aren't *many/some/any* animals in this circus.
6 I got *some/a/the* job.
7 We're buying *some/a lot of/many* furniture tomorrow.
8 Have you heard *any/the/a few* news?
9 We didn't eat *any/much/many* chocolate last Christmas.
10 I haven't spoken to *a lot of/many/much* people today

Reading

4 a How are the pictures connected? Read the text to find out, and choose the best title.

- Farmers' Food Is Too Hot For Elephants
- The Elephants' Party
- Dead Elephants Don't Eat Chilli

Mfuwe, Zambia, is a farming area. In 2004, the farmers had a problem: they lived near some elephants. Every few days these elephants ran over the farmers' land and destroyed a lot of food. Normally, when this happens, farmers shout at the elephants. When they hear a lot of noise, elephants get frightened and leave. The farmers tried this many times, but it didn't work.

So Mr Samson Banda, a farmer, decided to do something different. He put some hot chilli on his fence. When they came to his farm, the elephants hated the smell of the chilli and they stopped attacking Mr Banda's land. Other farmers copied his idea, and it worked for them too. Now some of them have started to grow chilli, and Mr Banda travels around Zambia telling farmers about his idea.

b Mark the sentences true (T) or false (F).

1 There were some elephants near the farms in Mfuwe.
2 The elephants ate all the farmers' food.
3 The farmers shouted at the elephants.
4 Mr Banda worked on a farm.
5 Elephants like the smell of chilli.
6 Mr Banda's plan was successful.
7 The other farmers didn't like his idea.
8 Some farmers in other parts of Zambia know about Mr Banda's idea.

Writing

5 Write two sentences using *although*.
the ostrich is a bird/can't fly

a *Although the ostrich is a bird, it can't fly.*
b *The ostrich is a bird, although it can't fly.*

1 parrots can talk/can't understand language
a _____ .
b _____ .

2 the exocoetidae is a fish/can fly
a _____ .
b _____ .

3 tigers are related to lions/are no tigers in Africa
a _____ .
b _____ .

4 chimpanzees can't talk/can communicate in sign language
a _____ .
b _____ .

Listening

6 **a** **10.3** Cover the tapescript and listen. Mark the sentences true (T) or false (F).
The speaker says:

1 in Europe and the US, dogs often live with families.
2 in Africa, dogs usually live in the house.
3 in Asia, an American advertisement was very successful.
4 in India, elephants have to work.
5 Africans love elephants.

b Read the tapescript. Find synonyms (words with the same meaning) for these words. The synonyms are underlined.

1 types _____
2 scared _____
3 it was not a success _____
4 dirty _____

c Here are seven adjectives. Find their opposites in the tapescript.

1 small _____
2 safe _____
3 weak _____
4 clean (2 words) _____
5 lovely _____
6 serious _____

> **TAPESCRIPT**
>
> Countries have different opinions of animals and different traditions. One example is dogs. In Europe and America, dogs are pets. They live in the house. They're part of the family. In other countries, in Africa and Asia, dogs are dirty animals. They live on the street. I remember an advertisement a few years ago, an American advertisement. It showed a man running with his dog. Man and dog as best friends. Well, they tried to show this advertisement in Asia and it was a <u>disaster</u>. No one wanted to see a man with a horrible, <u>unclean</u> animal like a dog. Another example is the elephant. In Europe, we love elephants. We think they're funny. In India, the elephant isn't funny at all. It's a worker. Elephants are used in all <u>kinds</u> of work because they're so strong. And then in Africa, elephants are killers. Every year they kill hundreds of people. They're big, dangerous animals and people are <u>frightened</u> of them.

Reading

1 Match the questions to the answers.

1 What do whales eat?
2 What do kangaroos wear in winter?
3 What keys do you find in trees?
4 What is a snake's favourite lesson?
5 Where do sick horses go?
6 What do you call a deer with no eyes?
7 What's the difference between a lion with a broken leg and a wet day?

a Hisssssstory.
b One roars with pain and the other pours with rain.
c Monkeys.
d No idea (no-eye deer).
e Jumpers.
f Fish and ships.
g The horsepital.

Vocabulary | animal sounds

2 Put the underlined letters in order to make animal noises.

Bears lwgor when they are hungry. *growl*
1 Our dogs sometimes abkr all night. _____
2 I love listening to my cat urrp. _____
3 When I hear snakes sihs, it frightens me! _____
4 The arro of a lion is the greatest sound in the jungle. _____
5 Wolves lowh when there is a full moon. _____
6 I think I heard a mouse keausq. _____

Vocabulary | verb + preposition combinations

3 Complete the sentences using words from the box.

> appeals   worries   listen   depends   agree
> responding   apply   spent

1 Did you _____ to the radio programme yesterday?
2 He _____ about his daughter because she's very lazy.
3 She _____ $45 on this dress.
4 I _____ with Boris. Let's go home.
5 When did you _____ for the job?
6 This book _____ to adults and children.
7 She isn't _____ to treatment.
8 I think we'll play today, but it _____ on the weather.

4 Choose the best words to complete the text.

> **Pets for Christmas? No, thanks**
> In the week after Christmas, thousands of pets are left on the streets – with no home and no food. Why? Because people buy pets for Christmas, and then change their minds. Pets (1) _____ to many people – the young and the old. But Chris Laurence, the chief vet for the RSPCA, says it is important to remember the cost of looking (2) _____ animals for the rest of their life. Pets are expensive. It depends (3) _____ the type of pet you have but, generally, people with pets (4) _____ £9,600 on a dog during its life, £8,000 on a cat and £7,600 on two rabbits. John Martin, a vet from Dublin, says, 'I agree (5) _____ people who say pets are good for us. Pets are friends for old people and they help children to grow up. But we have to listen (6) _____ what the RSPCA is saying. If you (7) _____ about your child's ability to care for animals, don't buy a pet.'
> If you want to (8) _____ to this article, write to petsindanger@blue.org.uk.

1	**A** help	**B** work
	C appeal	**D** give
2	**A** after	**B** to
	C for	**D** with
3	**A** of	**B** to
	C in	**D** on
4	**A** spend	**B** cost
	C buy	**D** pay
5	**A** to	**B** on
	C that	**D** with
6	**A** because	**B** for
	C to	**D** on
7	**A** nervous	**B** possible
	C worry	**D** frightened
8	**A** talk	**B** write
	C respond	**D** discuss

Grammar | *the*

5 Complete the sentences with *the* or nothing (–).

1 _____ cats are good pets.
2 _____ best pets are dogs because they are friendly.
3 What's _____ name of your rabbit?
4 This is _____ bird I told you about.
5 This is _____ cat that ate my fish!
6 _____ tigers are the biggest animals in the cat family.
7 Do you like _____ cats?
8 _____ horse we saw earlier is called Red Rum.
9 Is it true that _____ elephants have good memories?
10 _____ tallest animals are giraffes.

6 Complete the text with *the* (x7).

HOW TO LOOK AFTER YOUR PET SNAKE!

Snakes don't need much space. A strong box with small holes makes best home. Put paper or towels on the floor of box. Nicest climate for snakes is 80-85°F, and snake should be in direct sunlight, not artificial light. Put a large bowl of water in box. This is for snake to bathe, not drink. For meals, give the snake dead animals. Animals that are still alive sometimes fight and can cause problems. Most delicious animals for your snake are mice, frogs and lizards. Don't forget to tell your visitors that you have a pet snake!

How to ...

7 **a** Put the words in order to make sentences about the pictures.

> **Animals in the year 2100 AD**
> A group of 10-year-old children drew the animals of the future. Look at three of the best pictures.

1 type be it lion a of could

_____

Picture __
2 it like horse a looks

_____

Picture __
3 bird it's a perhaps

_____

Picture __
4 big it's I a think cat

_____

Picture __
5 a could it robot be

_____

Picture __
6 dangerous looks it

_____

Picture __
7 bird it's don't I think a

_____

8 doesn't animal like an it look

_____

9 isn't perhaps lion a it

_____

10 a couldn't it horse be

_____

b Which pictures are sentences 1–6 about?

Vocabulary | transport

1 Put the <u>underlined</u> letters in order to make forms of transport. Then put the words in brackets into the correct form to complete the sentences.

Sarah *took* (take) a <u>bus</u> <u>sub</u> to the main square.

1 I prefer _____ (ride) a _____ <u>cibelyc</u> around the city. It keeps me fit.

2 We had to show our tickets before _____ (get) on the _____ <u>rinat</u>.

3 We should _____ (catch) a _____ <u>xiat</u> to the airport, or we are going to _____ (miss) the _____ <u>nealp</u>.

4 Should I _____ (get off) the _____ <u>ubs</u> at the next stop for the museum?

5 We _____ (take) a _____ <u>ryefr</u> to Robin Island. It was beautiful.

6 We _____ (go) by _____ <u>acohc</u> to Amsterdam. It was cheaper than the train.

7 You have to pay if you want to _____ (drive) a _____ <u>rac</u> in the city centre.

8 He started _____ (ride) a _____ <u>botmoreki</u> when he was fifty.

Grammar | Present Perfect with *just, yet, already*

2 Correct the word order in the sentences.

Jim hasn't found yet a new job.

Jim hasn't found a new job yet.

1 We've come back from Turkey just, so we haven't seen your letters.

_____

2 Fernando already has had his lunch.

_____

3 A: Have you yet read that book?
  B: Yes, I've finished it just.

_____

4 A: Have yet you been to the museum?
  B: Yes, we've been there already.

_____

5 Already I have spoken to the manager about the problem.

_____

6 A: Is Roberto still there?
  B: No. He's left just.

_____

7 It is only 9.30, but Sam already has gone to bed.

_____

3 Look at the list of things Julia needs to do before she catches her plane. Write sentences to describe what Julia has done already (✓) or hasn't done yet (✗).

Things to do:

✓1 collect plane tickets
✗2 pack clothes
✓3 find passport
✓4 change money
✓5 buy sunglasses
✗6 close windows
✗7 water the plants
✓8 write Erica a letter with instructions
✗9 take the cat to Erica's house

1 *She has already collected the plane tickets.*
2 _____.
3 _____.
4 _____.
5 _____.
6 _____.
7 _____.
8 _____.
9 _____.

Pronunciation

4 **a** Choose the correct sound for the <u>underlined</u> letters.

1 Can I have a glass of orange <u>j</u>uice, please? /j/ or /dʒ/

2 Have you seen the Cathedral <u>y</u>et? /j/ or /dʒ/

3 I put the milk in the fridge. /j/ or /dʒ/

4 He's going to be a law<u>y</u>er. /j/ or /dʒ/

5 That shop sells lovely <u>j</u>ewellery. /j/ or /dʒ/

6 You'll need to ask the <u>j</u>udge. /j/ or /dʒ/

b [11.1] Listen and check your answers. Practise saying the sentences.

Vocabulary | holidays

5 Complete the sentences below. Use the words to complete the crossword.

```
        1                   2
 3  L  O  C  A  L
            4         5
        6         7
 8
            9
```

Across

3 You can see more of the city if you use _____ transport.

6 During busy periods it's best to _____ your holiday early.

8 We like museums and churches so we go _____ and take lots of photos.

9 Did you use buses and trains or _____ a car?

Down

1 I'm a good cook, so I enjoy self-_____ holidays.

2 I love discos, so every night I go _____.

4 I usually lie on a beach and _____ all day.

5 When I go on holiday I always _____ a towel, suncream and shorts.

7 The cheapest holidays are last _____ deals.

Lifelong learning

6 Complete the vocabulary notebook with the opposite words.

1 cheap (little money) vs ____ (lots of money)
eg The hotel was very cheap/____.

2 busy (lots of people/noise) vs ____ (no people/noise)
eg I walked through the busy/____ market.

3 empty (no people) vs ____ (lots of people in a place)
eg The room was empty/____.

How to ...

7 a Put the words in order to make sentences.

1 friend with mine an went I old of
_____

2 all We day sunbathed
_____

3 holiday on been I've just
_____

4 in stayed hotel beautiful We a
_____

5 got early deal and We a booked good
_____

6 was Greece a holiday two-week It beach in
_____

b Match the functions to the sentences in Ex. 7a.

a When? _____

b Who with? _____

c What/Where/How long? _____

d Where to stay? _____

e Booking? _____

f Activity? _____

Vocabulary | greetings and presents

1 Complete the sentences with a suitable word.

1 She _____ me on both cheeks when we said goodbye.

2 We bought some chocolates as a _____ to say thank you.

3 At the end of the concert the pianist _____.

4 We _____ at the aeroplane from the departure lounge.

5 The Prime Ministers _____ hands.

Grammar | verbs with two objects

2 Choose the best alternative.

1 He *told/promised* me a box of chocolates.

2 We *offered/owed* him a lift in our car.

3 Can you *bring/lend* me €100 until next week?

4 I have *sent/told* the questionnaire to the organisers.

5 The man in reception *told/gave* me a map.

6 My friend Pablo *brought/offered* me Spanish lessons.

7 The company *owes/tells* a lot of money to the employees.

8 I *told/gave* Julia's secret to everybody in the class.

3 Match the sentence halves.

1 I wrote
2 He bought
3 My father taught
4 Can I offer
5 I have lent
6 I promised
7 I told
8 Did you bring
9 Dave owes

a us some chocolate from Switzerland?
b you a cup of coffee?
c me €20 for the gas bill.
d me Portuguese.
e him the price of the new car.
f a letter to the bank this morning.
g her my CD player, because hers is broken.
h to give him a new bicycle for his birthday.
i me some flowers, and asked me to marry him!

How to ...

4 Add the words in brackets to these generalisations.

1 Italians love eating ice cream. (the)

_____

2 Children watch too much television. (tend to)

_____

3 Students have to get jobs in their holidays. (usually)

_____

4 Rich are getting richer every day. (the)

_____

5 People in Australia spend a lot of time outside. (generally)

_____

6 British eat a lot of roast beef. (the)

_____

7 Japanese workers don't take much holiday. (tend to)

_____

8 Teenagers don't listen to jazz or classical music. (usually)

_____

Listening

5 **a** `11.2` Cover the tapescript. Listen to some advice. Number the pictures in the order they are talked about.

b Listen again and complete the tapescript.

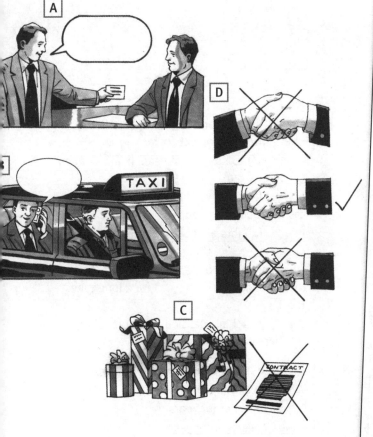

TAPESCRIPT

Advice 1: The ^{1} _____ tend to be very punctual in business. For any business meeting, you should arrive ^{2} _____, or even early. If you know that you'll be late, you should ^{3} _____ and tell someone about your delay.

Advice 2: When people meet for business, they ^{4} _____ introduce themselves by shaking hands. When you ^{5} _____, don't press too hard, or too lightly. A firm handshake is best.

Advice 3: People don't always exchange business cards when they meet. But if you need contact information, it is OK to ask a colleague for their ^{6}_____. It is also OK to ^{7} _____ someone your card. But you don't have to exchange cards, as in some cultures.

Advice 4: It's important not to offer ^{8} _____ or other presents as a way to help finalise a business deal.

Reading

6 Read Greg's diary and choose the correct answers.

Tuesday 14th September

What a terrible mistake! I've tried to do everything right since arriving in Russia, and now I've made a stupid mistake. Yesterday, Dimitri gave me some advice about how to behave in Russia. He explained that Russians are very polite. 'You should always offer to help a lady,' he explained. 'Gentlemen should pour drinks, and open doors, and do other things to help them.'

So last night when I went out to dinner with Nicolai, and his wife, Yulya, I wanted to do my best. At the end of the meal I offered Yulya a banana from the fruit basket. She smiled, and accepted, but she didn't take one. I didn't know what to do, so I picked a banana, peeled it and handed it to her. Yulya and Nicolai both smiled so I thought I had done the right thing. I told everyone at the hotel that in Russia, the polite thing is to peel bananas for the ladies.

But now I've learned my mistake. Grigorii has just told me that in Russia, when a man peels a banana for a lady it means he has a romantic interest in her. I feel so embarrassed.

1 Greg is
   A in the USA.
   B in Russia.

2 Greg gets some advice about
   A what to do in Russia.
   B Russian restaurants.

3 Dimitri says that gentlemen should
   A always offer to help ladies.
   B always invite ladies out to dinner.

4 When he goes out to dinner, Greg
   A eats Yulya's banana.
   B peels a banana for Yulya.

5 Greg thinks he has done the right thing because
   A Yulya and Nicolai smile at him.
   B Yulya peels a banana for him too.

6 Greg learns that in Russia if a man peels a banana for a lady it means
   A that he has a romantic interest in her.
   B that he likes bananas.

Grammar | Past Perfect

1 Choose the correct alternative.

The boy who kept walking

When 13-year-old Edward Daniel Sabillion arrived at New York's La Guardia Airport, he was tired. He (1) walked/had walked for 37 days from Honduras across Guatemala, Mexico, Texas and Florida.

Sabillion said his mother, brother and grandfather (2) died/had died in a disaster in Honduras. He had travelled to New York to find his father, who he (3) never met/had never met before.

When Edward arrived he (4) didn't find/hadn't found his father because he had lost the address and telephone number his father (5) sent/had sent him. The boy (6) spent/had spent a day at a police station. New York Police Captain, Thomas Kelly, said, 'He (7) ate/had eaten McDonald's and had some ice-cream cake.'

A few days later....

The truth comes out

Yesterday, Edward Sabillion finally (8) told/had told the truth about his story. He (9) didn't walk/hadn't walked for 37 days, from Honduras to New York. He already lived in the US, and had run away from home. His grandmother said she didn't know why he (10) invented/had invented this story, and she wanted him to come home.

2 Complete the sentences. Put the verbs in brackets into the correct form.

I *went* (✓) to Russia last year. I *hadn't been* (✗) before. (go)

1 I _____ (✓) very well because I _____ (✗) at all the night before. (sleep)

2 I _____ (✓) lots of photos on the last day because I _____ (✗) many before. (take)

3 I was very pleased that we _____ (✓) Jessica the other day, as I _____ (✗) for a long time. (see)

4 We _____ (✓) in a delicious restaurant. I _____ (✗) there before. (eat)

3 Answer the questions using the prompts.

Why didn't you recognise her?

I / not see / her for years

I hadn't seen her for years.

1 Why did you leave so early?

I / promise / to visit a friend

_____

2 Why was the house so quiet?

We / go / to bed

_____

3 Why didn't you eat with them?

I / have / my breakfast already

_____

4 Why didn't you stay in the hotel?

I / not book / a room

_____

5 Why didn't you buy the suit?

I / forgot / my credit card

_____

Pronunciation

4 **a** **11.3** Listen. Are *had* and *hadn't* stressed or unstressed?

b Practise saying the sentences.

Writing

5 **a** Put two words from the box in each circle.

> shy exciting crowded mountainous
> sunny friendly green comfortable
> tasty regular delicious cloudy

City

11 _____

12 _____

People

1 _____

2 _____

Countryside

9 _____

10 _____

Travel

Weather

3 _____

4 _____

Food

7 _____

8 _____

Transport

5 _____

6 _____

b Read the texts. What are they about?
Choose from the six categories in Ex. 4a.

1 When it came down, it came down hard, with a sound like stones hitting the roof. Needles of water were flying out of the black sky. Within minutes the road became a river.

2 I've been on gondolas in Venice, European trains, even a helicopter that circled New York, but this was the best journey of all. We saw cows in the street, people with baskets of food on their shoulders, sleeping dogs, whole moving markets, as one thin boy with bandy legs pulled our rickshaw.

3 The River Basayat, in front of us, snakes around the Charkandar Hills. If you look hard enough, you can see birds sky-dancing at the top of the mountain. There the trees are just matchsticks, the people tiny dots.

c Use the vocabulary in Ex. 4a to complete the sentences, making them more interesting.

1 We arrived at the _____ market.

2 There were _____ faces smiling from every corner.

3 A _____ girl walked past with a basket of flowers. She looked at her feet.

4 An old lady sold her _____ salads, ready to eat.

5 We drove in a _____ taxi through the _____ city centre.

6 The weather was good, so we enjoyed a _____ lunch on the _____ balcony, and looked at the _____ view.

Vocabulary | money

1 Complete the sentences with a word from the box in the correct form.

> withdraw win earn lend
> save borrow

1 Can you _____ me some money? I left my wallet at home.

2 I _____ £50 in a competition yesterday!

3 Can we stop at the bank? I need to _____ some money.

4 I _____ €50 an hour in my job.

5 We had to _____ money to pay for the car.

6 My sister _____ money every month. I spend mine immediately!

2 Choose the best words to complete the texts.

Memo: Advice for employees going to work in the UK
To: All
From: Jan
Work: you will earn a (1) _____, which is paid every month. You have to pay (2) _____ and this goes to the government. When you retire (aged 65), you get a (3) _____. In Britain you pay (4) _____ on money that you borrow from banks.
Shopping: most shops now take credit cards, but if you buy something in a market you usually pay in (5) _____. In small shops and on buses, etc. it's best to have the correct (6) _____. In restaurants, it is common to leave a (7) _____ of about 10% for good service.

	A		B		C	
1	A	cost	B	salary	C	price
2	A	for	B	pension	C	tax
3	A	tip	B	spending	C	pension
4	A	for	B	interest	C	price
5	A	cash	B	time	C	money
6	A	change	B	cost	C	price
7	A	money	B	tip	C	cheque

Grammar | second conditional

3 Complete the sentences using the words in brackets.

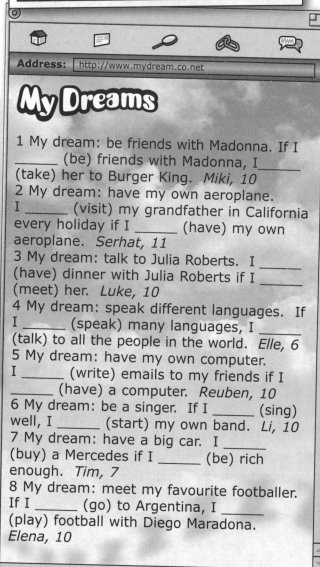

Address: http://www.mydream.co.net

My Dreams

1 My dream: be friends with Madonna. If I _____ (be) friends with Madonna, I _____ (take) her to Burger King. *Miki, 10*

2 My dream: have my own aeroplane. I _____ (visit) my grandfather in California every holiday if I _____ (have) my own aeroplane. *Serhat, 11*

3 My dream: talk to Julia Roberts. I _____ (have) dinner with Julia Roberts if I _____ (meet) her. *Luke, 10*

4 My dream: speak different languages. If I _____ (speak) many languages, I _____ (talk) to all the people in the world. *Elle, 6*

5 My dream: have my own computer. I _____ (write) emails to my friends if I _____ (have) a computer. *Reuben, 10*

6 My dream: be a singer. If I _____ (sing) well, I _____ (start) my own band. *Li, 10*

7 My dream: have a big car. I _____ (buy) a Mercedes if I _____ (be) rich enough. *Tim, 7*

8 My dream: meet my favourite footballer. If I _____ (go) to Argentina, I _____ (play) football with Diego Maradona. *Elena, 10*

4 Match 1–6 to a–f and write sentences using the second conditional.

1 If I/be/better at football   1
2 If she/not be/so busy
3 If she/know/his number
4 If I/not already have/a dog
5 If he/eat more   5
6 If I/live/in Brazil

a get/a cat.
b not be/hungry all the time.
c have to/speak Portuguese.
d have/time to see us.
e play/in the first team.
f call/him.

Bomdia.

5 Correct the mistakes in the sentences.

1 If I had more time, I'd to learn a new language.
2 What would you do when you lost your wallet?
3 If I would have a holiday, I'd go to Mauritius.
4 We wouldn't driven to work if we lived nearer the office.
5 She'd be here now if it is possible.
6 If you left your country, you would miss it?
7 I would sleep all morning if I would have the chance.
8 If I wasn't be so lazy, I wouldn't enjoy beach holidays.

Reading

6 **a** Read the stories. Then look at the sentences. Write N (Nathan), W (woman), NW (both), or X (neither of them).

1 __ found a lot of money.
2 __ travelled on a train.
3 __ gave some money back.
4 __ stole some money.
5 __ ran somewhere.
6 __ wrote a cheque.
7 __ spent a lot of money.
8 __ called the police.
9 __ did something wrong more than fifty years ago.
10 __ won some money.

The most honest boy in Britain

Nathan Gittings is the most honest boy in Britain. Nathan was standing at a bus stop when he found over £10,000 in cash in two shopping bags. At first he didn't do anything. He thought that someone would return for them. But the following day, the bags were still there. Nathan picked them up and ran home. He showed his mother what he had found and called the police.

Nathan said, 'I couldn't believe it when I found the money. I'd never seen that much in my life. But it wasn't mine so I knew I had to hand it in.'

The Gwent police were happy and surprised at Nathan's honesty. It was discovered later that the money belonged to a 'confused man'. It was his life savings.

The most honest woman in Britain

A woman who didn't pay for her train ticket returned to the station and paid for it ... fifty years later. The woman, now in her sixties, said she was late when she arrived at the station in 1950. She ran into the station and jumped onto the train. She wanted to buy a ticket on the train but no one came to check tickets that day.

Fifty years later the woman wrote a letter and sent a cheque to First North Western Railway Company. A single ticket is now £69 so she sent a cheque for £70. She had recently become religious and wanted to be honest about her past. The money will be given to charity.

b What do these words refer to?

1 them (*line 5*)
   a two shopping bags b the bus stop c the police
2 it (*line 11*)
   a his home b the bags c the money
3 it (*line 19*)
   a the train b the station c the ticket

Vocabulary | education

1 Look at the table and answer the questions.

	MATHS	GEOGRAPHY	HISTORY
Juan	94%		12%
Brigitte		92%	90%
Alessandra	6%		76%

1 Who took the Geography exam? _____
2 Who passed the Maths exam? _____
3 Who failed the Maths exam? _____
4 Who has to retake the History exam? _____
5 Who got two very good results? _____

2 Choose the best alternative.

1 Did you hear the exam *results/rewards?*
2 My favourite *subjects/topics* are: History, Geography and Biology.
3 I have to *fail/retake* my exam in June.
4 She attended most of her university *lectures/lessons.*
5 I *took/passed* my exam with a grade A.
6 I saw my old English *professor/teacher* from junior school yesterday.

Grammar | reported speech

3 Mick and Lola are talking. Put the sentences into reported speech. Use the verbs in brackets and *that.*

Mick: Lola, I'm hungry! (tell)
Mick told Lola that he was hungry.

1 Lola: You can go and buy some bread.
Lola _____. (tell)

2 Mick: I don't have any money.
Mick _____. (say)

3 Lola: That's nothing new.
Lola _____. (tell)

4 Mick: I'll go to the bank.
Mick _____. (say)

5 Lola: You don't have a bank account.
Lola _____. (tell)

6 Mick: I'm going to open a bank account.
Mick _____. (say)

7 Lola: You're going to need a job first.
Lola _____. (tell)

8 Mick: I'm not hungry any more.
Mick _____. (say)

4 Read the messages. What exact words did the speakers say?

John said he couldn't come tonight
'I can't come tonight.'

1 Rupesh said he would meet John at home at 6.
_____

2 Mary told me that her sister wasn't going to Germany.
_____

3 Rob said that my dinner was in the oven.
_____

4 Katia Scarfoni said she had been too busy to visit Renzo yesterday.
_____

5 Stephanie told me she had a meeting at 10.30.
_____

6 Dad said he had taken the keys.
_____

7 Mum said we could buy some milk.
_____

8 Suleiman told me the car was ready.
_____

5 These are the last things these people said before they died. Put their words into reported speech.

'I have no plans.' (Ramsay MacDonald, British Prime Minister)

He said that he didn't have any plans.

1 'That was the best ice-cream soda I ever tasted.' (Lou Costello, US comedian)

_____

2 'That was a great game of golf.' (Bing Crosby, US entertainer)

_____

3 'Luisa, you always arrive just as I am leaving.' (Massimo Azeglio, Italian politician, to his wife)

_____

4 'I'm bored.' (Gabriele D'Annunzio, Italian poet)

_____

5 'It has all been most interesting.' (Lady Mary Montagu, English writer)

_____

6 'Dying is the last thing I will do.' (Lord Palmerston, British politician)

_____

7 'Last words are for stupid people who haven't said enough.' (Karl Marx, German political theorist)

_____

How to ...

6 Put the words in order to make answers to the questions.

1 A: Do you earn a lot of money?
  B: say I'd not rather

_____

2 A: Are you into cricket?
  B: mean what , do you sorry ?

_____

3 A: Where will you be next year?
  B: question a that's good

_____

4 A: Do you think your team will win the championship this year?
  B: to difficult it's say

_____

5 A: What would you do if this happened to you?
  B: I it moment for think can a about?

_____

Writing

7 **a** Complete the expressions with the correct words from the box.

about   send   recently   could   grateful

1 I _____ saw your . . .
2 I'd be _____ if you could . . .
3 Could you _____ me . . .
4 I'd like to know more _____ . . .
5 _____ you tell me . . .

b Write the expressions from Ex. 7a in the correct place in the letter.

4 Clarendon Road
West Gorlip
SE2 7BC

Dear Mr Garvey,
1 _____ advertisement in the *Hounslow Chronicle*, and I am very interested in the Russian language course.
2 _____ the course, for example, 3 _____ how much it costs? Also, 4 _____ let me know what time it finishes, because I pick up my children from school at 4.00. Anyway, 5 _____ an information pack? My address is as above.

Yours sincerely,
Cecilia Rowntree

Vocabulary | verbs + prepositions

1 The <u>underlined</u> prepositions in the sentences are wrong. Correct them.

1 I like listening <u>at</u> music. _____

2 I applied <u>to</u> a job in Jamaica. _____

3 Look <u>with</u> the horses! _____

4 Do you argue <u>to</u> your brothers a lot? _____

5 I apologised <u>to</u> being late. _____

6 We waited <u>up</u> you for twenty minutes. _____

7 Maybe we'll have a picnic, but it depends <u>for</u> the weather. _____

8 I paid <u>to</u> the drinks by credit card. _____

9 Do you want to play <u>by</u> your friends? _____

2 Put the lines of the email in the correct order.

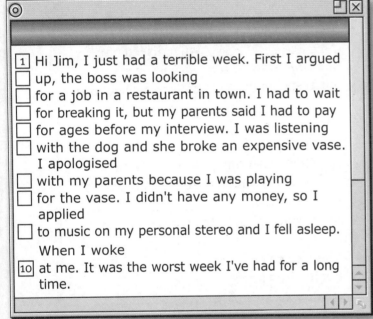

```
[1] Hi Jim, I just had a terrible week. First I argued
[ ] up, the boss was looking
[ ] for a job in a restaurant in town. I had to wait
[ ] for breaking it, but my parents said I had to pay
[ ] for ages before my interview. I was listening
[ ] with the dog and she broke an expensive vase.
    I apologised
[ ] with my parents because I was playing
[ ] for the vase. I didn't have any money, so I
    applied
[ ] to music on my personal stereo and I fell asleep.
    When I woke
[10] at me. It was the worst week I've had for a long
    time.
```

Grammar | both / neither / either

3 Look at photos A and B of American presidents. Are these sentences true (T) or false (F)?

1 Both of them are with their wife. [T]

2 Neither of them is wearing a tie. [ ]

3 Bill's child isn't in the photo and John's isn't either. [ ]

4 Neither of them has got a beard. [ ]

5 Both their wives are wearing a hat. [ ]

6 I don't think either of them looks unhappy. [ ]

7 Both of them have got short hair. [ ]

8 Neither of the presidents is wearing a suit. [ ]

A

4 Complete the sentences with *both*, *neither* or *either*.

The Strange Story of Two Presidents

1 Abraham Lincoln worked on a boat. John F. Kennedy also worked on a boat.

_____ of them worked on boats.

2 Lincoln was killed while he was President. Kennedy was also killed while he was President.

_____ Lincoln nor Kennedy finished their presidency.

3 Lincoln became President in 1860. Kennedy became President in 1960.

They _____ became presidents in the sixties.

4 Lincoln studied law, but didn't work as a lawyer. Kennedy also studied law, but didn't work as a lawyer.

_____ of them worked as lawyers.

5 Many white people in the south didn't like Lincoln. Many white people in the south didn't like Kennedy.

Many white southerners didn't like _____ them.

6 After Lincoln died, Andrew Johnson (born 1808) became President. After Kennedy died, Lyndon Johnson (born 1908) became President.

Men called Johnson followed _____ of them.

7 Lincoln was killed in Ford's Theatre. Kennedy was killed in a Ford Lincoln car.

_____ of them died in Fords.

8 Kennedy saw a ghost of Lincoln in the White House (but this might not be true).

There is _____ a ghost of Lincoln in the White House or someone invented the story.

Listening

5 **a** [12.1] Cover the tapescript. Zeinab and Rob have finished a Spanish course. Number the ideas in the order they talk about them.

Do exercises on the Internet. ☐

Read Spanish books and newspapers. ☐

Listen to cassettes. ☐

Write emails to a Spanish friend. [1]

Do a conversation exchange. ☐

Travel to a Spanish-speaking country. ☐

TAPESCRIPT

R: Zeinab, are you going to continue with your Spanish?

Z: Oh yes, definitely.

R: How? What are you going to do?

Z: That's a good question. I've got lots of ideas. I've got a Spanish friend and we write emails to each other. We always wrote in English, but now we can write in Spanish.

R: That's great.

Z: And I'm hoping to visit her in Madrid too, so I can practise my Spanish. What about you?

R: I want to find someone to do a conversation exchange.

Z: What's that?

R: Conversation exchange? It's when you find, say, a Spanish person who wants to improve their English. Then you meet. And you speak together for half an hour in English and half an hour in Spanish.

Z: That's a good idea.

R: Yeah. I hope I can find someone at a language school.

Z: Do you read much?

R: Yeah, I like reading.

Z: I want to try reading books in Spanish.

R: What type?

Z: I'm going to try short novels or children's books. Maybe newspapers too.

R: Good idea. And there's always the Internet. There are lots of websites for language learners.

Z: That's true. And cassettes too, to improve your listening.

R: Yeah, we've got the cassettes from the course.

---

b Mark the sentences true (T) or false (F).

1 Zeinab wants to write emails to a friend in English.

2 Zeinab wants to visit her friend in Madrid.

3 Rob wants to do a conversation exchange with a Spanish speaker.

4 Rob and Zeinab don't like reading.

5 Zeinab wants to read poetry in Spanish.

6 They have listening cassettes from their Spanish course.

Pronunciation

6 **a** [12.2] Tick (✓) the sentences from each pair that you hear.

1 a Either of us will win.

  b Neither of us will win.

2 a Both boys bought a bag.

  b Beth's boys bought a bag.

3 a They're either French or Spanish.

  b They're neither French nor Spanish.

4 a He saw us both.

  b He saw the boats.

5 a It's either blue or grey.

  b It's neither blue nor grey.

6 a We're most interested in art.

  b We're both interested in art.

b Listen and repeat the sentences.

The definite article (*the*) and phrasal verbs

1 Complete the sentences by adding one missing word.

1 When I was in Mexico I picked a little Spanish.
2 This is man who I told you about.
3 When she was a child she looked up her father.
4 John Brown grew in a big, happy family.
5 Golf is best sport in the world.
6 I was brought on a farm, so I've always loved animals.
7 There are two cinemas here – cinema on Brand Street is very small.
8 I've found a great restaurant – I came across when I went for a walk yesterday.
9 Jack was most intelligent student I've ever taught.
10 I have to after my little sister because she's feeling sick.

Countable/uncountable nouns

2 One alternative in each sentence is incorrect. Cross it out.

1 I had *a bit of / a lot of / many* work to do yesterday.
2 We didn't want *much / many / any* information.
3 There are *a few / a little / some* jobs I would never do.
4 I saw the same article in *much / a lot of / a few* newspapers last week.
5 I hope to do *some / any / a bit of* travel in the future.
6 We didn't know there were *any / many / much* animals in the Amazon.
7 I asked for *a little / many / some* advice about which subjects to study.
8 Have you heard *many / much / any* news about the election results?
9 Did you find *a bit of / any / a few* furniture for the new office?
10 I wrote *a little / some / a lot of* cheques last week.

Present Perfect with *just/yet/already*

3 Complete the gaps with *just, yet* or *already*.

1 I haven't seen the film _____. (I'm seeing it tomorrow.)
2 She's _____ done her homework. (She did it two days early.)
3 Have you _____ heard Jamelia's new CD? (I expect you have.)
4 My sister has _____ had a baby boy! (She had him two hours ago.)
5 Has David _____ finished? (The test only started ten minutes ago.)
6 I've _____ met my new boss. She's beautiful! (I met her one minute ago.)
7 We've _____ studied this topic. (We studied it weeks ago.)
8 She hasn't decided what to eat _____. (She is very slow to choose.)
9 They've _____ opened a new school. (They opened it this morning.)
10 My cousins have _____ visited me. (I didn't expect them so soon.)

Past Perfect

4 <u>Underline</u> the best verb form.

1 We visited Syria. We *didn't go / hadn't been* there before.
2 I went to Bill's house but he wasn't there. He *went / had gone* into town already.
3 She switched off the television and *went / had gone* to bed.
4 I wanted to listen to my personal stereo but I *left / had left* all my CDs in the flat.
5 A new secretary arrived. She *didn't work / hadn't worked* in our office before.
6 I left my job in the hospital and after that I *worked / had worked* in a factory.
7 I didn't recognise Josie because I *didn't see / hadn't seen* her for years.
8 He heard music from the flat below. The party *started / had started* already.
9 It was Dr Luber on the phone! *Did he find / Had he found* a solution to their problem?
10 I got into the car and *drove / had driven* for hours. The road was quiet.

Second conditional

5 Make second conditional sentences using the verbs in brackets.

1 If I _____ (have) enough money,
I _____ (buy) an aeroplane.

2 She _____ (stay) here longer
if _____ (can).

3 If you _____ (not/work) here,
where _____ (like) to work?

4 The city _____ (be) perfect if
there _____ (not/be) so many cars.

5 _____ (you/do) a presentation at the
conference If we _____ (pay) you?

6 If laptop computers _____ (be) cheaper,
I _____ (get) one.

7 I _____ (not/sleep) if I _____ (drink)
as much coffee as Paola.

8 If everyone _____ (stop) smoking
we _____ (save) millions of euros every
year.

9 _____ (she/call) him if
she _____ (have) his number?

10 If I _____ (had) the choice,
I _____ (not/live) in a small town.

Reported speech

6 Change the sentences from direct speech to reported speech.

1 'We both like fish.'
They told me that . . .

2 'Neither of my brothers went to university.'
I said that . . .

3 'I can't dance.'
She told me that . . .

4 'It will rain later.'
He said that . . .

5 'I've lost my watch.'
He told me that . . .

6 'We don't have any money.'
They said that . . .

7 'I won't tell anyone your secret.'
She told me that . . .

8 'I'll either go to China or India for my holiday.'
He said that . . .

9 'Both of my dogs sleep all day.'
She told me that . . .

10 'Neither of my sisters has travelled much.'
I said that . . .

Vocabulary

7 a Complete the sentences using verbs from the box. You may have to change the verb form.

> appeal depend book pass worry
> shake miss apply retake spend

1 When you meet another businessman, you
should _____ hands.

2 That sounds great. A week on the beach
really _____ to me!

3 Hurry up! We're going to _____ the plane!

4 I read the advertisement, but I
didn't _____ for the job.

5 I'm so happy because I _____ all my
exams!

6 We _____ a lot of money on food.

7 I don't know if we'll go away this weekend.
It _____ on the weather.

8 If you fail, you have to _____ your exam.

9 You need to _____ your holiday early.

10 Don't _____ about the test. You'll do very
well.

b Complete the sentences using nouns from the box.

> subject cash transport tip salary
> race deal mouse pension lecture

1 She's been quiet as a _____ for the last hour.

2 Will you get a _____ when you retire?

3 The waiter was excellent. I'm going to leave
a _____ .

4 Did you go to the _____ about Picasso?

5 I'm leaving the city. I hate being part of the
rat _____.

6 What's your favourite _____ at school?

7 For our holiday we got a last
minute _____. It was really cheap.

8 When I'm abroad, I use local _____ to
travel around.

9 My _____ is paid every month into my
bank account.

10 I always pay in _____. I hate credit cards.

Vocabulary bank

Phrases with *go, have* and *get*

Put the phrases in the box in the correct place in the table. Add more phrases as you learn them.

> on well with someone   children   on a diet
> to bed late   by bus   better/worse   married
> in touch   a shower

go	clubbing
have	a lie-in
get	up early

Food and drink

Add more words to the word map as you learn them.

Drinks
mineral water
_____
_____
_____

Equipment
frying pan
_____
_____
_____

Tastes
delicious
_____
_____
_____

Food and Drink

Phrases
eat out
_____
_____
_____

Other
spaghetti
_____
_____
_____

Food

Vegetables
carrots
_____
_____
_____

People
chef
_____
_____
_____

Fruit
raspberries
_____
_____
_____

Describing people and places

Complete the words in the chart. Add more words or phrases as you learn them.

Describing people (appearance)

th_____

tal_____

good-lo_____

overwei_____

skin_____

Describing people (character)

determ_____

ambit_____

hard-_____

organis_____

chat_____

Describing places

be situa_____ in

regi_____

landsc_____

natural beau_____

84

Jobs

Write the job in the correct place in the list. Add other jobs as you learn them.

> firefighter   secretary   sales rep
> receptionist   plumber   fashion designer

Who welcomes people to a building? _____
Who designs clothes? _____
Who fixes problems with water pipes? _____
Who travels around selling a product? _____
Who stops fires? _____
Who helps the boss get organised? _____

Verbs + prepositions

Write the verbs in the correct place according to the preposition. Add to the list as you learn more verbs + prepositions.

> depend   appeal   agree   respond   argue
> apply   spend (money/time)   listen   belong
> play   apologise   wait

_____	ON	_____	FOR
_____		_____	
		_____	
_____			
_____	TO	_____	WITH
_____			
_____			

Phrasal verbs

Put the correct preposition next to the verb. Add to the list as you learn more phrasal verbs.

> after   over   up   to   with   on   across   out

1 get _____ with = have a good relationship
2 go out _____ = be someone's partner
3 ask someone _____ = invite someone on a date with you
4 put _____ with = accept a bad situation without complaining
5 get _____ = stop feeling sad about something
6 look _____ = take care of
7 come _____ = find by chance
8 look up _____ = respect

Transport

Look at the picture. Add the different types of transport to the table below. Add other types of transport as you learn them.

Usually for one person	bicyle
Can take 1 - 5 people	
Usually takes many people	
Takes goods/things AND many people	train
Usually transports goods/things (not people)	

Answer key

Unit 1 24 hours

Lesson 1.1
Vocabulary: everyday actions

1 a 1 j 2 h 3 d 4 g 5 b 6 c 7 i 8 e 9 f 10 a

1 b 1 check my e-mails 2 chat on the phone 3 listen to the radio 4 catch a bus 5 stay in bed late 6 watch TV

Grammar: likes and dislikes

2 a 1 hate 2 love 3 keen 4 like 5 love 6 mind 7 like 8 stand 9 quite

3 1 like 2 don't mind 3 quite keen on 4 can't stand 5 really like 6 not very keen on

Reading

4 a Noon – Think about a problem 2 p.m. – Visit the dentist 5 p.m. – Eat your dinner 8 p.m. – Stretch

b 1 T 2 F 3 T 4 T 5 F 6 T

Vocabulary: time phrases

5 a 1 In 2 At 3 On 4 In 5 in 6 At/On 7 In 8 On 9 At

Lesson 1.2
Listening

1 a

	Sleep weekdays (hours)	Sleep weekend (hours)	Insomnia (yes/no)	Alarm clock (yes/no)
Liz	about six	about ten	no	yes (two)
Paul	seven or eight	six or seven	yes (sometimes)	no (not usually)

b 1 Liz 2 Liz 3 Paul 4 She can't sleep 5 Because she turns the first one off and falls asleep again 6 When he has to get up very early

Vocabulary: daily routines

2

Grammar: Present simple

3 1 doesn't know 2 finishes 3 lives 4 works 5 has 6 enjoys 7 doesn't smoke 8 does 9 doesn't work 10 spends 11 watches 12 reads 13 goes 14 does 15 doesn't cook 16 brings

4 1 A: Do you like swimming? B: Yes, I do. 2 A: Do they got to bed early every night? B: No, they don't. 3 A: Does she speak Spanish? B: Yes, she does. 4 A: Does he go to university? B: No, he doesn't. 5 A: Do you have lots of homework? B: No, I don't. 6 A: Do we have her telephone number? B: No, we don't. 7 A: Do they remember you? B: Yes, they do. 8 A: Do you want to come out later? B: Yes, I do.

Grammar: adverbs of frequency

5 1 I hardly ever forget to take my books to college. 2 Jake is never late. 3 We often see Pablo and Juan after the game. 4 Do you always drink coffee in the morning? 5 We sometimes visit my grandmother in France 6 It is usually sunny in August.

Pronunciation: *do/does*

6 b 1 A: What do you <u>do</u>? B: I'm an artist. 2 A: Do you like going to the cinema? B: Yes, I <u>do</u>. 3 A: Do you have the tickets? B: No, I <u>don't</u>. 4 A: <u>Does</u> she know we're coming? B: Yes, she <u>does</u>. 5 A: <u>Do</u> you remember your dreams? B: No, I <u>don't</u>. 6 A: Does he have a car? B: No, he <u>doesn't</u>.

Lesson 1.3
Vocabulary: everyday actions

1 1 Yes, he does No, he isn't. He's skiing. 2 Yes, they do. Yes, they are. They're playing guitar. 3 Yes, she does. No, she isn't. She's going to the cinema.

2 1 practise 2 teach 3 am dancing 4 are performing 5 think 6 work 7 don't have 8 like 9 are skiing 10 are staying 11 is 12 'm learning

3 1 don't like 2 are celebrating 3 finishes 4 'm not watching 5 's having 6 isn't working 7 doesn't think 8 's looking

Reading

4a The future of shopping

b 1 a 2 b 3 c 4 b 5 c 6 a

Writing

5 business (line 5) realy (line 11) finnish (line 13) traveling (line 15) planing (line 16)

Unit 2 Music

Lesson 2.1
Vocabulary: music

1 a 1 lead singer = picture b 2 composer = picture d 3 band = picture a 4 guitar = picture f 5 concert = picture e 6 compilation cd = picture c

b 1 c 2 e 3 d 4 b 5 f 6 a

Grammar: Past Simple

2 1 sang 2 was 3 won 4 used 5 studied 6 met 7 was 8 changed 9 died 10 started 11 became 12 performed 13 sold

3 1 What did you eat for lunch? 2 Where were you this morning? 3 What did you do on Saturday night? 4 When did you leave school? 5 When did you start this job? 6 What instrument did you play at school? 7 Where did you live as a child? 8 What did you study at college?

4 1 didn't like 2 had 3 didn't sleep 4 ate 5 didn't go 6 was 7 didn't see 8 lived 9 didn't do 10 gave

Pronunciation

5 1 played 2 washed 3 worked 4 ended 5 hated

6a a ago b in c as d after e up f of g at

b 1 e 2 g 3 c 4 f 5 b 6 d 7 a

Lesson 2.2
Vocabulary: word families

1 1 tiredness 2 intelligence 3 relaxing 4 tired 5 relaxation 6 energetic 7 imagination 8 relaxing 9 energy

2a

1	Oo	tiring
2	Ooo	energy
3	oOo	relaxing
4	ooOo	energetic
5	oOoo	intelligent
6	oOooo	imaginative
7	oooOo	imagination

Grammar: *So do I/Neither am I*

3 1 j 2 c 3 f 4 h 5 e 6) b 7 i 8 a 9 g 10 d

4 1 So did I. 2 I don't. 3 So have I. 4 Neither can I 5 So do I 6 I don't 7 I didn't 8 I'm not 9 So do I

Listening

5a

	Jazz	Rock	Dance	Classical
Pavel	✓	✓	✓	✗
Helena	✓	✗	✗	✓

b 1 into 2 listened 3 bands 4 music 5 to 6 really 7 would 8 read

Lifelong learning

6b stress (1)   example sentence (4)   definition (3)   part of speech (2)

Writing

7 I like many different types **of** music. Hip hop is my favourite, but I also listen **to** rap music. My favourite band is call**ed** Fugees. I love their CD, The Score – the songs are intelligent and have excellent tunes. Sometimes I **listen** to classical music. I like Verdi and Puccini. I don't go **to** concerts because I prefer listening to music at home.

Lesson 2.3

Grammar: Present Perfect

1 1 I've made 2 I've performed 3 I've won 4 have you sold 5 I've sold 6 Have you 7 have you changed 8 haven't changed

2 1 haven't watched 2 haven't been 3 haven't tasted 4 haven't played 5 haven't read 6 haven't met

3a 1 arrived 2 sold 3 has changed 4 started 5 became 6 has won 7 watched 8 has been

b 1 M 2 C 3 M 4 H 5 C 6 H 7 M 8 H

Vocabulary: achievements

4 I was born in Denmark in 1980 and I started playing the violin when I was 3 years old. When I was 12, I **won** a prize for Young Musician of the Year. I came to England to study music. I also **learned** English. I **passed** my music exams in 1997 and **travelled** to the United States to play with an orchestra. I **wrote** articles for the 'New York Musician' magazine and **made** speeches at many music colleges. In 2004 I **started** my company MusiciansExchange.com. The company organises international travel for music students.

Reading

5a 1 NO, G 2 G 3 NO, G, S 4 S 5 NO, G, S 6 S

b Salzburg: it = the Salzburg Music Festival; its = the salzburg Music Festivals. New Orleans: the city = New Orleans; its = jazz; them = the 350 people. Glastonbury: there = at Glastonbury; it = Glastonbury.

c 1 It 2 Its 3 They 4 They 5 its

Unit 3 Taste

Lesson 3.1
Vocabulary: food, drink, people, kitchen equipment

1 1 h 2 i 3 j 4 l 5 k 6 e 7 f 8 a 9 g 10 b 11 c 12 d

2 1 cook for myself 2 cut down on 3 a vegetarian 4 celebrity chef 5 on a diet 6 dinner party 7 eat out 8 gave up

Listening

3a summary 2: Hannah is a vegetarian who likes eating at home.

b 1 When she was at school. 2 No, she doesn't. 3 Yes, she does. 4 She does. 5 From cookery programmes on television. 6 Italian 7 No, she isn't. 8 She is on a diet.

Vocabulary: phrases

4 1 chef 2 restaurant 3 tasty 4 success 5 experience 6 abroad

Grammar: *going to*

5 1 She's going to leave her job. 2 We're going to win the World Cup. 3 They're going to play on the beach. 4 I'm not going to be a doctor. 5 He's going to pass his exam(s). 6 They aren't going to get married.

6 1 are going to sell 2 's / is going to start 3 Are the builders going to finish 4 's / is going to have 5 aren't going to have 6 Are you going to visit 7 're / are going to try 8 'm / am not going to be

How to ...

7 1 A: <u>Where</u> are you going for your holidays? B: We're going <u>to</u> visit my cousins in South Africa 2 A: What <u>are</u> your plans for next year? B: <u>I'm</u> going to look for a job because I need to earn some money. 3 A: What <u>are</u> you going to do at the weekend? B: I'm going <u>to</u> stay at home <u>on</u> Saturday to study. 4 A: What are <u>your</u> plans for when you leave university? B: <u>I'm going</u> to work abroad.

Lesson 3.2
Reading

1a *Fast Food, Fast Women* – negative *My Big Fat Greek Wedding* – positive

b 1 F 2 T 3 F 4 T

c 1 has a date with 2 kids 3 movie 4 accept

Pronunciation

2a 1 My <u>daughter</u> hurt her <u>knee</u>. 2 The <u>writer thought</u> about her book. 3 It was a cold <u>night</u> in <u>Autumn</u>. 4 There were <u>eight</u> <u>foreigners</u>. 5 <u>Could</u> you take the dog for a <u>walk</u>? 6 I <u>know</u> you're <u>wrong</u>. 7 The <u>sign</u> was <u>high</u> in the sky.

b

Silent *g*	Silent *w*	Silent *l*	Silent *k*	Silent *n*
daughter	writer	could	knee	autumn
thought	wrong	walk	know	
night				
eight				
foreigners				
sign				
high				

Grammar: relative clauses

3a Down **1** who **2** which **3** who **4** which **7** which **8** which
Across **5** which **6** where **9** where **10** who

b

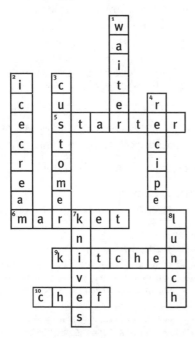

4 **1e** A builder is someone who builds houses. **2f** A cooker is a machine which makes food hot. **3g** An airport is a place where people catch planes. **4a** A pilot is someone who flies planes. **5d** A pencil is something which you use for writing or drawing. **6b** An author is someone who writes books. **7h** A cinema is a place where you can watch films. **8c** A menu is something which tells you what food you can eat.

Lifelong learning

5 **1** It's something which you use for opening bottles. **2** It's the thing that you use to dry yourself. **3** It's the stuff which you can put on bread. **4** It's the thing which you use for changing the TV programme. **5** It's something that you can cook in. **6** It's the white stuff that you put on your food.

Writing: informal letters

6a Dear Anna,
Thanks for your letter. I'm sorry I didn't reply sooner, but I only received the letter this morning. I have been away on holiday with my sister, and I only came home yesterday. We went camping in Cornwall, which was beautiful except for the weather. It rained nearly every day!
It's very kind of you to invite me to stay. I would love to come to Scotland, and it would be great to see you again. We haven't seen each other for nearly two years now – I can't believe it. I could come for the last weekend in September (27th / 28th). I am finishing my job, so I will have a few days free. Would that be OK with you?
Anyway, I hope you're well, and I am looking forward to hearing your news. How is your course going? Are you still planning to open a flower business when you finish?
Speak to you soon.
Love,
Paola

Lesson 3.3
Vocabulary

1 **1** Did you make this chocolate cake? It's very tasty / absolutely delicious! **4** I don't think the soup is very good. It's a bit tasteless. **5** That meat looks absolutely horrible. I think it's old.

2 **1** location **2** high **3** appearance / texture **4** appearance / texture **5** dishes **6** quality

3 **1** sounds horrible **2** smells old **3** feels so soft **4** tastes delicious **5** looks expensive

Grammar

4 **1** A: are you doing B: I'm staying ... watching **2** A: Are you cooking B: We're having **3** A: Are you doing B: I'm not playing ... it's raining. **4** A: are you getting B: 'm not driving ... 'm catching ...

5 A: Are you coming B: 're bringing **6** 're not going / aren't going ... A: 's going **7** aren't arriving **8** A: Are you coming ... B: I'm not working ...

5 **1** 're / are going **2** 're / are leaving **3** 'm / am visiting **4** 's / is meeting **5** Are you playing ...? **6** We're not moving **7** 's having / is having **8** Are they catching...? **9** 're / are working **10** 's finishing

How to ...

6a

Sal	Bella
Plans: *staying at home*	Plans (Sat): *going to a concert*
Reason: *to study for her exams*	Reason: *Diane bought tickets*
	Plans (Sun): *going to Oxford*

b **1** Sal is staying at home to study for her exams. **2** On Saturday, Bella is going to a concert. **3** On Sunday, Bella is going to Oxford.

c Conversation 1
(2) Hello Jim. **(8)** Thanks Jim. I'll tell you ... **(4)** Not really. I am staying at home to study for my exams. **(1)** Hello Sal. It's Jim. **(7)** OK. I'll call you again next week. Good luck with your exams! **(6)** Oh, that's really nice of you but I don't like going out when I have to study. I'm sorry. Perhaps another time? **(3)** Are you doing anything this weekend? **(5)** I see. Well, why don't you come out for a drink on Saturday evening? There's a new bar opening on the river...
Conversation 2
(3) What are you doing on Saturday evening? **(1)** Hello, Bella? It's Jim. **(7)** Perfect! I can meet you on the river at 7pm. **(4)** Nothing. Why? **(8)** 7.30 would be better for me. I'm going to Oxford on Sunday to visit my aunt and I'm driving so I won't be back ... **(5)** Well, would you like to come out for a drink, or something to eat? **(2)** Hello. **(6)** Great idea! Oh, wait a minute. Saturday? No, I've just remembered. I'm going to a concert on Saturday. Dianne's bought some tickets to see Guns and Roses. Why don't we go out on Sunday evening?

Review and consolidation units 1-3
Present Simple vs Present Continuous

1 **1** Are you leaving **2** doesn't usually wear **3** never watch **4** is James talking to **5** Do you know **6** sometimes goes **7** am looking **8** often has lunch **9** are you doing **10** isn't raining

2 **1** What do you do? f **2** Where are you going? e **3** What is she eating? j **4** Where do they live? or Where are they living? c **5** What time do you get home? g **6** Are you going to the shops? a **7** What is Paul doing? i **8** Are you enjoying your course? h **9** How do you get to work? d **10** Does Jayne have a car? b

Present Simple vs Present Perfect

3 **1** started **2** have made **3** sold **4** have won **5** have toured **6** have they been **7** have always loved **8** started **9** sang **10** was **11** have always been

4 **1** A: Have you ever been to Brazil? B: Yes. I went to Carnival in Rio last year. **2** A: I have lived in Rome for five years now. B: Why did you move there? **3** A: Did you visit any interesting sights in Beijing when you were there? B: No. We didn't have enough time. **4** A: Have you ever seen any famous bands in concert? B: I saw Pink Floyd when I was a teenager. **5** A: Did you watch the Spiderman film on television last night? B: No. I have seen it three times already.

Going to and Present Continuous
(for future plans/arrangements)

5 **1** We **are** leaving on Friday at 2 p.m. **2** Are you go**ing** to see Tariq this weekend? **3** I'm hav**ing** lunch with my mother tomorrow. **4** We **are** meeting in Hyde Park. **5** **Are** they coming to the party tonight? **6** I'm **not** flying to Hong Kong. **7** He is **going** to buy a new computer later. **8** We aren't go**ing to** drive through the mountains. **9** Is Mark playing football on Saturday? **10** Maria isn't **coming** to the restaurant.

Defining relative clauses

6 **1** where **2** who **3** which **4** which **5** where **6** where **7** who **8** which **9** where **10** which

7 **1** I can't find that bag which you gave me. **2** Are these the keys which you can't find? **3** Do you remember the restaurant where we met **4** Do you know the name of that hotel which has double rooms for 50 euros? **5** That's the woman who offered me her seat on the bus. **6** My sister introduced me to a man who has his own software company.

Vocabulary

8 **1** food: delicious, disgusting, get a takeaway pizza, lamb, mineral water, onion, tasty, vegetable, yoghurt **2** daily routine: fall asleep, get up early, read a magazine **3** shops: customers, products, shop assistant, staff **4** music: classical, compilation CD, concert, go clubbing, lead singer, play the violin, **5** adjectives: energetic, intelligent

9 **1** cook **2** nap **3** picnic **4** into **5** download **6** relaxed **7** started **8** tasty **9** checked **10** distinction

Unit 4 Survival

Lesson 4.1
Vocabulary

1 **1** breath **2** physical strength **3** mental **4** controlled **5** rely **6** achieved **7** challenge

Grammar: comparatives

2 **1** more expensive than **2** better accommodation than **3** more enjoyable than **4** friendlier than **5** longer **6** greater variety than **7** younger than **8** fitter than

3a **1** This one isn't as fast **as** the other one. **2** It was much **worse** this morning. It rained for hours. **3** It was **more** interesting than his last one, and I liked the acting. **4** This one is **cheaper** than the other place, and breakfast is included. **5** She's **crazier** than her sister. **6** It's better than my last one because I have more independence.

b **1** cars **2** weather **3** films **4** hotels **5** people **6** jobs

4 **1** D **2** S **3** S **4** D **5** D **6** S

5 **1** is bigger than **2** more dangerous than **3** as difficult as **4** isn't as important **5** old as **6** deeper than

Vocabulary: adjectives to describe people

6

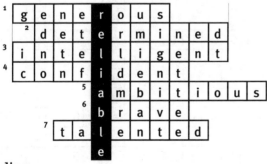

Reading

7 **1** F **2** F **3** T **4** F **5** F **6** T **7** T **8** T

Lesson 4.2
Vocabulary: survival

1 **1** b **2** e **3** a **4** f **5** c **6** d

2 **1** challenges **2** skills **3** shelter **4** cope **5** myself **6** wilderness

Grammar: superlatives

3 **1** I've watched some boring films, but this is the most boring. **2** I've had some bad days, but this is the worst. **3** I've played in some great games, but this is the greatest. **4** I've lived in some quiet places, but this is the quietest. **5** I've stayed in some expensive hotels, but this is the most expensive. **6** I've had some long conversations, but this is the longest. **7** I've learned some important lessons, but this is the most important. **8** I've had some crazy moments, but this is the craziest.

4 **1** the strongest **2** the most intelligent **3** the best **4** the smallest **5** the hardest **6** the most popular **7** the tallest **8** the fittest

5 **1** is the fastest **2** best food I have ever **3** of the easiest **4** the most popular **5** most beautiful house I have **6** the smallest theatre in **7** is the heaviest **8** the best

Pronunciation

6a **1** F **2** D **3** A **4** B **5** C **6** E

b **1** The **big**gest **day** of your **life** **2** The **best** **book** of the **year** **3** The **tast**iest **snack** of the **day** **4** The **fun**niest **pro**gramme on **TV** **5** The **fast**est ma**chine** on the **road** **6** The **hot**test **show** in **Lon**don

Writing

7 **1** B **2** C **3** C **4** A **5** B **6** A **7** D

Lesson 4.3
Grammar: indirect questions

1 **1** what the time is **2** where I can find an Internet cafe **3** where the nearest tube station is **4** what time the next train leaves **5** if the museum is open on Sunday **6** how much a ticket costs **7** how far it is to the airport **8** where I can buy a phonecard

2a **1** Can you tell me what I can do if a snake bites me? **2** Do you know if mobile phones work in the Amazon? **3** Do you know how much the plane ticket costs from London? **4** Can you tell me where the nearest airport is? **5** Do you know if there is a hotel in the Amazon? **6** Can you tell me how far the nearest town is? **7** Do you know if I can drink the water from the river? **8** Can you tell me if I need any injections before I go?

b a 4 b 5 c 3 d 8 e 1 f 6 g 2 h 7

Listening

3a **1** Dialogue 1 = Camden Market **2** Dialogue 2 = Buckingham Palace **3** Dialogue 3 = Tate Modern **4** Dialogue 4 = Regent's Park **5** Dialogue 5 = Indian restaurant, Brick Lane **6** Dialogue 6 = Paddington Station

b **1** closes **2** About **3** if **4** Enjoy **5** if **6** sign **7** nearest **8** about **9** what **10** try **11** leaves **12** over

Reading

4a **1** F **2** F **3** T **4** T

b **1** a **2** a

Unit 5 Stages

Lesson 5.1
Vocabulary: stages of life

1 **1** *teenager* (n) **2** elderly (adj) **3** middle-aged (adj) **4** baby (n) **5** old (adj) **6** child (n) **7** adult (n) **8** toddler (n) **9** pensioner (n)

2

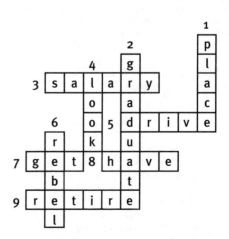

Grammar: should(n't), can('t) and (don't) have to

3a **1** can't **2** don't have to **3** have to **4** shouldn't **5** don't have to **6** can **7** can't **8** should **9** have to **10** shouldn't **11** should **12** have to

b **1** Diane: fashion designer **2** Clive: footballer **3** Rafael: businessman **4** Siegfried: dentist

4 **1** I can't look after the children today. **2** Do you have to work at weekends? **3** Should we go to the shop this morning? **4** I have to buy a new guitar. **5** I can swim very well. **6** You shouldn't play there. It's dangerous. **7** Can you help me with my bags? **8** I don't have to do any homework tonight.

5 **1** C **2** A **3** A **4** D **5** C **6** A **7** D **8** C

Pronunciation

6 **1** You shouldn't go home. **2** We can't see very well. **3** You have to do the shopping. **4** Can't you read? **5** We should watch this. **6** I don't have to work tonight. **7** Should he call me? **8** I can understand it. **9** They have to come.

How to …

7 **1** A: In my opinion, you need a haircut. B: I don't think so. **2** A: What do you think? B: You look … interesting. **3** A: We need to clean this room. B: You're probably right. **4** A: Beautiful scenery. Don't you think so? B: I'm not so sure.

Lesson 5.2
Reading

1 **1** CS **2** S **3** CS **4** N **5** CS **6** CS **7** C **8** CS

b **1** b **2** c **3** a **4** d

Grammar: Present Perfect with for and since

2 **1** I haven't been to the cinema (a) for ages (b) since June (c) ~~since years~~. **2** We haven't played tennis (a) since last year (b) ~~ages ago~~ (c) for months. **3** She's worked here (a) for two weeks (b) ~~since three months~~ (c) for a long time. **4** I've played the piano (a) since I was a child (b) ~~since ages~~ (c) for five years. **5** Have you lived here (a) for a long time? (b) since January? (c) ~~years ago?~~ **6** Has she known him (a) for years? (b) since last July? (c) ~~for February?~~ **7** I haven't seen you (a) since I was in India (b) for a year or two (c) ~~since months~~. **8** He's been in the team (a) ~~since two weeks~~ (b) since he scored his first goal (c) for too long.

3 **1** here since last **2** has lived here for **3** known John since **4** hasn't smoked for **5** haven't seen Giorgio since **6** have played tennis since **7** have been here for **8** written poetry for

4 **1** have they lived **2** He has been **3** I haven't smoked **4** I haven't seen **5** have you known **6** She has had **7** We haven't spoken **8** has he worn

Vocabulary: friendship

5 **1** a **2** b **3** c **4** a **5** c **6** c

Writing

6 **S**ince university I've worked as a sales representative for a publishing company. **I**t's a nice job. **M**y colleagues are really friendly and **I** travel a lot. **A**t the moment I'm living in **M**ilan. I've been here two years and **I** love the city. **I**'m not married. **I** haven't been in touch with anyone from university for years but **I**'d love to hear from you, so send me an email.
Sandy Smith

Lesson 5.3
Reading and listening

1a A Long, Long Life

b long life, home town, smoke cigarettes, feel stressed, sense of humour, ride a bike, grow old, get bored, true story, amount of money

c **1** long life **2** home town **3** smoked two cigarettes … drank red wine **4** felt stressed / got bored **5** sense of humour **6** rode a bike **7** grew old **8** true story **9** amount of money

Grammar: used to

2a **1** Did you use to watch a lot of TV? **2** Did you use to go abroad for your holidays? **3** Did you use to cook for your parents? **4** Did you use to help your mother around the house? **5** Did you use to do a lot of exercise?

b **1** e **2** c **3** d **4** a **5** b

3 **1** Did you use to work here? **2** I used to eat junk food. **3** Didn't she use to be a singer? **4** She didn't use to smoke so much. **5** Did you use to get on well with your grandparents? **6** We used to have to work all the time. **7** I didn't use to listen to the radio. **8** We used to have a house on the beach.

Listening

4a

IS NOW		USED TO BE
A	supermarket	a school
B	car park	a sports field
C	museum	a hospital
D	Old Pool Hotel	a swimming pool

b **(1)** used to be **(2)** didn't use to be **(3)** used to be **(4)** use to be **(5)** didn't use to

Vocabulary: good and bad habits

6

key   word

	1	h	e	a	t	h	i	l	y

(crossword)

1 h e a t h i l y
2 f o o d
3 s m o k e r
4 p h y s i c a l
5 a c t i v e
6 l a t e
7 w a t e r
8 p o s i t i v e l y

Unit 6 Places
Lesson 6.1

Vocabulary: geography

1

(crossword)
2 I t a l y
3 P o r t u g a l
4 S w i t z e r l a n d
5 S l o v
6 J a p a n
7 G r e e k
9 C a
10 G e r m a n y
11 S p a n i s h
12 P o r t u g u e s e
1 C a n a d a
8 E u r o p

2 **1** island **2** ocean **3** river **4** mountain **5** forest **6** beaches **7** desert **8** lake **9** Sea

Grammar: will

3 **1** will carry **2** won't be **3** will pay **4** won't sleep **5** will show **6** won't know

4 **1** I'll see **2** I'll go **3** Will you stay **4** I'll finish **5** I'll get **6** I do **7** I visit **8** I'll send

Pronunciation: /ɒ/ and /əʊ/

5

/ɒ/ – orange	/əʊ/ – won't
shop	closed
sorry	no
clock	don't
shopkeeper	open
promise	only
got	most
	home
	know

Reading

6 1 S 2 W 3 W 4 S 5 W

7 1 NI 2 T 3 F 4 F 5 T 6 NI

8 1 e 2 c 3 b 4 f 5 d 6 a

Lesson 6.2
Grammar: too/enough/many

1 1 too 2 too many 3 enough 4 too much 5 too 6 enough
7 too much 8 too many

2 1 too loud 2 tall enough 3 too many suitcases 4 enough
money 5 too crowded 6 too small

3 1 too tired 2 hard enough 3 too much time 4 too expensive
5 too many hamburgers 6 good enough 7 too long 8 too many
people 9 too busy 10 old enough

Vocabulary

4 1 mobile phone 2 vacuum cleaner 3 CD player 4 freezer
5 answer phone 6 radio 7 hair dryer 8 dishwasher

How to...

5 1 should / because 2 'd like / couldn't 3 to choose /
main 4 take / too 5 go / because

Listening

6a Summary 1

b 1 interesting 2 technology 3 mobile telephones
4 programme 5 teenagers 6 television 7 confusing
8 car parks

Lesson 6.3
Grammar

1 1 Would you like 2 Do you like 3 would like
4 would you like 5 Do you like 6 'd like

2 1 look like 2 don't like 3 likes 4 like 5 's he like
6 am I like 7 'd like

b Man A – Marc, Man B – speaker

3 1 look like 2 like 3 Would you like 4 does it look 5 is it
6 Would you/'d like 7 does he look 8 Do you like
9 is 10 What's it

Pronunciation

4 1 <u>What</u> do you like <u>doing</u> at the <u>weekend</u>? 2 <u>What</u> would you
like to <u>do</u> this <u>evening</u>? 3 <u>What's</u> your <u>mother</u> like? 4 <u>What</u> does
she <u>look</u> like? 5 Do you <u>like</u> <u>swimming</u>? 6 Would you <u>like</u> some
<u>help</u>?

Reading / Listening

5b 1 A man was drinking coffee in his **garden**. 2 An **old**
couple walked past and asked if they could buy his washing
machine. 3 The old man only had **$10**. 4 They bought the
washing machine for $2.50. 5 Later, the man sold his fridge to
a family with **five** children and a dog. 6 Then he sold his **video
player**, his hairdryer and his sofa. 7 He had **$8.70**. 8 When a
young boy returned with his dog, the old man told him that he was
the **richest** man in the world.

Writing

6a 1 there: in the garden 2 it: the washing machine 3 it:
$10 4 his: the dog's name 5 it: the fridge

b 1 It was beautiful. 2 The people who live there are lucky.
3 I love watching it. 4 It felt like we were the only people there.

Review and consolidation units 4-6
Comparatives and superlatives

1 1 hotter 2 more dangerous 3 the largest 4 younger
5 more interesting 6 the most romantic 7 smaller 8 the best
9 lazier 10 the prettiest 11 kinder 12 the fastest

Indirect questions

2 1 Can you tell me what time the bus leaves? 2 Can you tell
me how much these shoes cost? 3 Do you know who the 41st US
President was? 4 Can you tell me how this photocopier works?
5 Do you know what the capital of Mexico is? 6 Do you know when
the next train leaves? 7 Can you tell me if the museum is open on
Sundays? 8 Do you know if there is a train to Asiago?
9 Can you tell me if Josh works here? 10 Do you know if Penguins
fly?

should(n't), can('t), (don't) have to

3 1 I **can fly** an aeroplane. 2 We **should buy** our tickets early.
3 You **don't have to** pay for children. 4 She **has to do** her exam
again. 5 **Can I go** home now? 6 We s**houldn't arrive** late. 7 She
can't drive. 8 Do we **have to read** this book? 9 You **should eat**
more vegetables. 10 Do **I have to** leave?

used to and Present Perfect with for and since

4 1 I **used to smoke** but I haven't had a cigarette **since** last year.
(c) 2 She **used to be** good at the guitar but she hasn't played **for**
two years. (e) 3 We **didn't use to like** each other when we were
children but we've been friends **for** the last few months. (a) 4 Mum
and Dad **used to travel** a lot but they haven't had a holiday **since**
1999. (d) 5 I **didn't use to cook** much pasta but I've eaten a lot of it
since I went to Italy. (b)

will with too/enough/very

5 1 will be / too 2 will you have / very 3 won't stay / too
4 will they arrive / very 5 very / won't need 6 will study /
enough 7 too / will rain 8 very / won't be 9 will you go / very
10 won't go / too

like/would like/be like/look like

6 1 Would you like a drink? g 2 Does she look like her sister? d
3 What do you like doing in your free time? e 4 What is John's
girlfriend like? f 5 Where would you like to go tomorrow? h
6 Who do you look like? b 7 Does your brother like Ireland? c
8 What is that book like? a

Vocabulary

7 1 adult 2 brave 3 challenge 4 desert 5 elderly 6 forest
7 generous 8 healthily 9 intelligent 10 junk 11 kit 12 lose
13 middle-aged 14 nightlife 15 ocean 16 pensioner
17 questions 18 rely 19 smoker 20 talented 21 umbrella
22 video recorder 23 washing machine 24 young 25 Zealand

Unit 7 Body

Lesson 7.1
Vocabulary

1 1 waist 2 shoulder 3 elbow 4 wrist 5 ear 6 nose
7 back 8 knee 9 finger 10 cheek 11 ankle 12 eye
13 mouth 14 hair

2 1 like 2 put 3 on 4 makes 5 appearance

3 1 short 2 overweight 3 tall 4 thin 5 well-built
6 muscular 7 medium height 8 skinny 9 tall 10 handsome
11 good-looking

b 1 muscular 2 overweight 3 handsome 4 tall
5 medium-height 6 skinny

4a **1** wai **ST** omach **2** mou **TH** in **3** wri **ST** ressed
4 handso **ME** dicine **5** sever **AL** ternative **6** ank **LE** ssons
7 sandwi **CH** eek **8** fa **CE** lebrity **9** mon **TH** umb

b **1** stressed **2** medicine **3** sandwich **4** waist **5** month
6 celebrity **7** several **8** lessons

Grammar

5 **1** we'll celebrate with a party. **2** we'll stay in and eat a
pizza. **3** I'll go to the bank and get some. **4** I'll buy you a copy
for your birthday. **5** we'll talk about it later. **6** there won't be any
left. **7** will you come?

6 **1** see / will you **2** don't come / will be **3** will be / don't
call **4** don't leave / 'll miss **5** won't be / go **6** find / we'll
7 'll be / aren't **8** don't sleep / won't feel

7 **1** If Pete does lots of exercise, his muscles will get stronger.
2 If Shaune does yoga, she will feel happier. **3** Their skin will look
better if they drink lots of water. **4** They will feel more relaxed if
they have massages every day. **5** If Shaune eats salads for a week,
she will lose weight. **6** They won't / will not feel so tired if they
sleep for 10 hours a day. **7** If they don't / do not smoke for a week,
they will feel healthier. **8** They 'll be / will be less stressed if they
don't / do not think about work. **9** If Pete loses weight, he will have
more energy.

Lesson 7.2
Vocabulary

1 **1** ambitious **2** chatty **3** organised **4** sensitive
5 hard-working **6** open **7** unreliable **8** reserved

Pronunciation
2

oOo	oO	Oo	Ooo
ambitious hard-working	reserved	chatty open	organised sensitive

Grammar

3 **1** to think **2** talking **3** meeting **4** to take **5** working
6 to change **7** moving **8** to find **9** to tell **10** seeing

4 **1** to learn **2** looking at **3** to read **4** to do **5** to try
6 to tell **7** to change **8** listening **9** to understand
10 to travel **11** winning **12** to say

5 **1** correct **2** I miss seeing my friends and family. **3** I expect
you to be here at 9 o'clock. **4** correct **5** He has decided to
take a week off work. **6** We avoided telling you earlier because
of your exams. **7** You can't afford to go out every night. It's too
expensive. **8** I promised to go to her house this evening. **9** I want
to tell you what happened. **10** correct

Reading

6b **1** B, C, D
2 A, D

7.3
How to...

1 **1** That's really funny. **2** I don't get it. **3** That's not very funny.

Vocabulary: illness and injury

2 **1** sprained wrist **2** sore throat **3** pain in my chest
4 high temperature **5** feel sick **6** broken leg

3 **1** Have you got an aspirin? **I've got** a terrible headache.
2 I can't eat anything. I feel sick. **3** You don't look well. **Have you
got / Do you have** a high temperature? **4** Steve is in hospital.
I think he's got **a broken arm.** **5** I'm going to try acupuncture for
my **backache.** **6** I don't feel very good. I've got **a cold.** **7** I'm
staying at home. I've **got** the flu.

Grammar: purpose/reason/result

4 **1** that **2** in order **3** because **4** to **5** so **6** not to
7 so that I **8** because it

5 **1** to **2** because **3** so that **4** to **5** because **6** so
7 so that **8** so that **9** to **10** so

Writing

6a **1** – C **2** – A **3** – B

b **1** c **2** b **3** f **4** e **5** g **6** d **7** a

Listening

7a **1** c.)

b

SHIATSU	
What are the main beliefs?	Like (1) acupuncture it believes that there are channels of (2) energy.
Where is it from?	It is a (3) Japanese massage.
What happens in a typical session?	• Firstly, the practitioner will (4) ask you questions about your health. • Then, he/she will give you a (5) massage. • Lastly, he/she will (6) press points on your body.
What does it treat?	It is very good for (7) backaches, stomachaches and (8) headaches.
How long does it take?	A session takes about (9) 1 hour.
Do patients always feel better immediately?	(10) No. Sometimes it takes (11) more sessions.

Unit 8 Speed

Lesson 8.1
Vocabulary: speed

1 **1** e **2** g **3** d **4** f **5** a **6** b **7** c
2 **1** in **2** behind **3** up with **4** on **5** down **6** up

Grammar: Present Simple passive

3 **1** are made **2** is written **3** is played **4** is stopped
5 am taken **6** is spent **7** are washed **8** am given

4 **1** What food is Italy known for? **2** What meat is not served to
Hindus? **3** How much milk is drunk in US compared to fizzy drinks?
4 What complaint is heard most often in US fast food restaurants?
5 Which animal is not eaten by Muslims? **6** How many teaspoons
of sugar are contained in one glass of cola?

Reading

5a **1** B **2** B **3** C **4** A **5** C

b **1** are delivered **2** are checked **3** are made **4** serves
5 gives **6** is given **7** is owned **8** is known

How to ...

6a **1** d **2** c **3** a **4** e **5** f **6** b

b **1** d = diagram D **2** c = diagram C **3** a = diagram E
4 e = diagram F **5** f = diagram B **6** b = diagram A

Lesson 8.2
Vocabulary

1 **1** asked him out **2** going out with **3** grow apart
4 put up with **5** split up **6** got over

2 **1** a **2** c **3** c **4** b **5** b **6** b

Grammar: questions

3 **1** To William Shakespeare: Where did you **get** your ideas from?
2 To Bart Simpson: Why **are you** yellow? **5** To Britney Spears: Can
you teach me **to sing** like you? **6** To Vincent Van Gogh: Why **did
you** cut off your ear? **7** To Quentin Tarantino: Why **are** your films so
violent? **8** To Pablo Picasso: Why **did** you **paint** people with three
noses?

4a 1 g **2** f **3** b **4** h **5** e **6** a **7** c **8** d

b A 8d **B** 7c **C** 4h **D** 2f **E** 1g **F** 5e **G** 3b **H** 6a

5 1 Where are you from? **2** What is your job? **3** What did you study? **4** What are your hobbies? **5** How many brothers and sisters do you have? **6** Have you done speed-dating before? **7** When are you going back to Germany? **8** Will you come back to England? **9** What do you think of speed-dating? **10** What are you reading at the moment?

Listening

6a

jobs	✔
the weather	
children	
family	✔
education	✔
clothes	
hobbies	✔

b
NOTES
Mr Marius Cecillon   Miss Judith Stein
Job: translator   works in a **bank**

Met in **Paris, four** years ago

Miss Stein studied **Economics** at New Mexico State University
Hobbies: goes to **the gym** in the **evening** 3 or 4 times a week

Lesson 8.3
Grammar: Past Continuous and Past Simple

1 1 I was watching TV when the lights went out. **2** She got up and had a shower. **3** Didn't you meet him when you were at university? **4** We were driving across France when the car broke down. **5** I found $10 while I was walking home yesterday. **6** He lost his wallet when he was playing with the children.

2 1 was watching **2** heard **3** was **4** didn't have **5** called **6** were listening **7** invited **8** was sitting **9** was **10** weren't **11** was walking **12)** didn't know **13** was studying **14** was reading **15** heard **16** went **17** didn't finish

3 see tapescript

Writing

4a 1 last summer **2** after a while **3** In the end **4** To begin with **5** So I decided **6** One night **7** suddenly

b 1, 6, 4, 2, 5, 7, 3

5a 1 Y **2** Y **3** DK **4** Y **5** N **6** DK

b 1 D **2** B **3** C **4** E **5** F **6** A

c 1 recovered **2** training **3** crowds **4** amazed **5** unconscious

Unit 9 Work

Lesson 9.1
Vocabulary

1 1 plumber (B) **2** mechanic (H) **3** lawyer (G) **4** accountant (D) **5** firefighter (C) **6** nurse (E) **7** factory worker (A) **8** a sales rep (F)

2 1 e **2** h **3** g **4** b **5** a **6** i **7** c **8** d **9** f

3 1 B **2** A **3** B **4** C **5** A **6** B **7** C **8** A **9** C **10** A

Pronunciation

4 1 qualifications **2** application form **3** experience **4** salary **5** interviewee **6** receptionist **7** Managing Director **8** factory **9** company **10** CV

Listening

5 1 BI **2** GI **3** GI **4** BI **5** BI

6 1 bad **2** two pages long or less. **3** lies **4** qualifications

5 write a new CV for each job **6** food **7** was given the job

Lesson 9.2
Vocabulary: *make* and *do*

1 1 He sits in his office all day **doing** absolutely nothing. **2** Have you **made** a decision about where to go on holiday? **3** She makes an effort to be friendly to all her employees. – correct **4** Can you **do** me a favour? **5** I have **done** a lot of research on the internet. **6** Good luck in the interview. You can only do your best. – correct **7** Have you **made** an appointment to see the doctor? **8** The food was cold so we **made** a complaint.

2 1 making progress **2** did research **3** done your homework **4** do a lot of business **5** making decisions **6** make an effort **7** made a complaint **8** makes a lot of money

Grammar: *can/could/be able to*

3 1 could speak **2** can't understand **3** could catch **4** couldn't sleep **5** can't sing **6** can't believe **7** can take **8** could hear **9** can finish **10** couldn't even cook

4 1 can't **2** can **3** be able to **4** could **5** can **6** be able to **7** can't **8** couldn't **9** Can **10** couldn't

Reading

5

	Special talent	When did he/she start?	Achievements or hopes for the future
Abigail Sin	Playing the piano	When she was two	Plays in Singapore Concert Hall
Ali Fukuhara	Playing table tennis	When she was three	Training for the Olympics
Nguyen Ngod Truong Son	Playing chess	When he was three	Won national tournaments. Wants to beat the grand masters of chess

Pronunciation

6a 1 U **2** U **3** S **4** S **5** U **6** U **7** S **8** S

Lifelong Learning

7a 1 d **2** e **3** f **4** a **5** b **6** c

Lesson 9.3
Vocabulary

1 1 The judge gave the criminal a 5-year prison sentence. **2** The thief stole a bicycle and had to pay a £100 fine as his punishment. **3** The police officer arrested a young woman. **4** The jury decided that the woman was innocent.

2a a thief **b** rob **c** burglar **d** mugging **e** pickpocket **f** shoplifter **g** murder

b 1 shoplift **2** burgle **3** pick someone's pocket **4** steal **5** murder **6** mug **7** rob

Grammar

3 1 was mugged **2** was arrested **3** was given **4** was taken **5** was robbed / took **6** decided **7** was stolen **8** was burgled **9** stole **10** was punished

4 1 was asked **2** bought / was given **3** left / was stolen **4** took **5** were told / started **6** Were you invited **7** was met **8** was driven

5 1 When was the vase stolen? **2** What time was it stolen? **3** Where was it stolen from? **4** Who reported it? **5** How much reward was offered? **6** Where was the vase found? **7** When was it returned?

Reading

6 1 Money. **2** He went to a shop **3** Three times **4** No, he wasn't **5** In the bin **6** To an Italian shop **7** He didn't have his glasses **8** To get his glasses and telephone the police **9** The manager **10** They arrested the failed robber

Writing

7a Introduction – 1, Story – 2 Conclusion - 3

b One-legged thief is caught.
A shopkeeper helped to catch a burglar who only had one leg.
Ghanshyam Patel, who is 56, fought with Eric Gardener, after Eric tried to rob him in the street.
During the fight, Ghansyam pulled off Eric's false leg by mistake, but then the thief escaped by hopping with one leg into his car.
However, later he tried to order a new leg, and the police arrested him. Gardener, 41, was jailed for three years after he said he was guilty.
Mr Patel said, ' It was a real shock when his leg came off in my hands.'

Review and consolidation units 7-9
First conditional

1 **1** will feel **2** finish **3** stops **4** passes **5** will be **6** don't have **7** go **8** don't fall **9** wants **10** will you come

Gerunds and infinitives

2 **1** going **2** to see **3** to change **4** moving **5** to help **6** to write **7** to see **8** meeting **9** to be **10** to buy

Present Simple passive

3 **1** are delivered **2** is cleaned **3** are built **4** is employed **5** isn't used **6** are made **7** are recycled **8** are sent **9** is done **10** is closed

Past Continuous vs Past Simple

4 **1** was raining / happened **2** came / was talking **3** were having / asked **4** was travelling / heard **5** was / was shining / were singing **6** was walking / met **7** was listening / didn't hear **8** was going / remembered **9** got / went **10** was watching

can/could/be able to

5 **1** be able to **2** can't **3** couldn't **4** could **5** can't **6** couldn't **7** be able to **8** could **9** can't **10** Can

Past Simple passive

6 **1** My bag was taken. **2** The thief was arrested. **3** The museum was built in 2001. **4** The President was met at the airport. **5** All their passports were checked carefully. **6** They were told about the delays. **7** All the work was finished over the weekend. **8** The employees were invited to the party. **9** He was asked to work seven days a week. **10** The piano was damaged when it was carried upstairs.

Vocabulary

7 **1** sore **2** skinny **3** handsome **4** hard-working **5** toe **6** flu **7** broken **8** ill **9** chatty **10** hurry

8 **1** work **2** arrive **3** asked **4** deteriorated **5** catch **6** run **7** applied **8** do **9** making **10** had

Unit 10 Wildlife

Lesson 10.1
Vocabulary: animals

1

t	i	g	e	r	w	o	l	f
e	l	e	p	h	a	n	t	
			e	a	g	l	e	
			c	o	w	c	a	t
			s	p	i	d	e	r
d	o	g		s	n	a	k	e
b	e	a	r	z	e	b	r	a
h	o	r	s	e				
h	y	e	n	a	l	i	o	n

2 **1** as quiet as a mouse **2** plenty more fish in the sea **3** eats like a horse **4** the rat race **5** have kittens **6** let the cat out of the bag **7** kill two birds with one stone

Vocabulary: phrasal verbs

3 **1** b **2** e **3** h **4** a **5** f **6** d **7** g **8** c

4 **1** grew up **2** gets on **3** looks up to **4** comes across **5** look after **6** take to

5 **1** you picked up **2** grow up in **3** you Ever come across **4** get on with **5** you take to **6** looking after your **7** look up to **8** brought up in

Pronunciation

6 **1** I grew <u>up</u> in <u>Bath</u>. **2** I <u>brought</u> her <u>up</u>. **3** I'll <u>look after</u> you. **4** I <u>look up to</u> my <u>Mum</u>. **5** I <u>came across</u> it. **6** I <u>picked</u> it <u>up</u>.

Lifelong Learning

7 • write a definition (3) • organise new words by topic (1) • write example sentences (5) • write if there is an object with new verbs (2) •write a translation (4)

8a **1** well **2** so, anyway **3** I mean **4** you see

c **1** d **2** a **3** b **4** c

Lesson 10.2
Grammar: countable and uncountable

1 **1** U **2** C **3** U **4** U **5** C **6** U **7** U **8** U

2 **1** much **2** Quite a lot **3** Not much **4** A few **5** many **6** a few **7** a lot **8** much **9** much **10** a lot **11** a few **12** none

3 **1** many **2** many **3** a few **4** a bit **5** some **6** some **7** many **8** a few **9** many **10** much

Reading

4a Farmers' Food Is Too Hot For Elephants

b **1** T **2** F **3** T **4** T **5** F **6** T **7** F **8** T

Writing: although

5 **1a** Although parrots can talk, they can't understand language. **b.** Parrots can talk, although they can't understand language. **2a** Although the exocoetidae is a fish, it can fly. **b.** The exocoetidae is a fish, although it can fly. **3a** Although tigers are related to lions, there are no tigers in Africa. **b.** Tigers are related to lions, although there are no tigers in Africa. **4a** Although chimpanzees can't talk, they can communicate in sign language. **b.** Chimpanzees can't talk, although they can communicate in sign language.

Listening

6a **1** T **2** F **3** F **4** T **5** F

b **1** types = kinds **2** scared = frightened **3** it was not a success = disaster **4** dirty = unclean

c **1** small – big **2** safe – dangerous **3** weak – strong **4** clean (2 words) – dirty, unclean **5** lovely – horrible **6** serious – funny

Lesson 10.3
Reading

1 **1** f **2** e **3** c **4** a **5** g **6** d **7** b

Vocabulary: animal sounds

2 **1** bark **2** purr **3** hiss **4** roar **5** howl **6** squeak

Vocabulary: verb + preposition combinations

3 **1** listen **2** worries **3** spent **4** agree **5** apply **6** appeals **7** responding **8** depends

4 **1** c **2** a **3** d **4** a **5** d **6** c **7** c **8** c

Grammar: the

5 **1** – **2** The **3** the **4** the **5** the **6** – **7** – **8** The **9** – **10** The

6 **How to look after your pet snake**
Snakes don't need much space. A strong box with small holes makes **the** best home. Put paper or towels on the floor of **the** box. **The** nicest climate for snakes is 80 – 85F, and **the** snake should be in direct sunlight, not artificial light. Put a large bowl of water in

the box. This is for **the** snake to bathe, not drink. For meals, give the snake dead animals. Animals that are still alive sometimes fight and can cause problems. **The** most delicious animals for your snake are mice, frogs and lizards. Don't forget to tell your visitors that you have a pet snake!

7 1 It could be a type of lion. Picture A   **2** It looks like a horse. Picture C   **3** Perhaps it's a bird. Picture B   **4** I think it's a big cat. Picture A   **5** It could be a robot. Picture B   **6** It looks dangerous. Picture ABC   **7** I don't think it's a bird.   **8** It doesn't look like an animal.   **9** Perhaps it isn't a lion.   **10** It couldn't be a horse.

Unit 11 Travel

Lesson 11.1
Vocabulary: transport

1 1 I prefer to ride a bicycle around the city. It keeps me fit.   **2** We had to show our tickets before getting on the train.   **3** We should catch a taxi to the airport, or we are going to miss the plane.   **4** Should I get off the bus at the next stop for the museum?   **5** We took a ferry to Robin Island. It was beautiful.   **6** We went by coach to Amsterdam. It was cheaper than the train.   **7** You have to pay if you want to drive a car in the city centre.   **8** He started to ride a motorbike when he was fifty.

Grammar: present perfect with *just, yet, already*

2 1 We've just come back from Turkey, so we haven't seen your letters.   **2** Fernando has already had his lunch.   **3** A: Have you read that book yet? B: Yes, I've just finished it.   **4** A: Have you been to the museum yet? B: Yes, we've already seen it.   **5** I have already spoken to the manager about the problem.   **6** A: Is Roberto still there? B: No. He's just left.   **7** It is only 9.30, but Sam has already gone to bed.

3 1 She has already collected the plane tickets.   **2** She hasn't packed her clothes yet.   **3** She has already found her passport.   **4** She has already changed some money.   **5** She has already bought some sunglasses.   **6** She hasn't closed the windows yet.   **7** She hasn't watered the plants yet.   **8** She has already written a letter for Erica.   **9** She hasn't taken the cat to Erica's house yet.

Pronunciation

4 1 /dʒ/   **2** /j/   **3** /dʒ/   **4** /j/   **5** /dʒ/   **6** /dʒ/

Vocabulary
5

Lifelong learning

6 1 expensive   **2** quiet   **3** crowded

How to …

7 a I went with an old friend of mine.   **b** We sunbathed all day.   **c** I've just been on holiday.   **d** We stayed in a beautiful hotel.   **e** We booked early and got a good deal.   **f** It was a two-week beach holiday in Greece.

b a3   b1   c6   d4   e5   f2

Lesson 11.2
Vocabulary: greetings and presents

1 1 kissed   **2** present / gift   **3** bowed   **4** waved   **5** shook

Grammar: verbs with two objects

2 1 promised   **2** offered   **3** lend   **4** sent   **5** gave   **6** offered   **7** owes   **8** told

3 1 f   **2** j   **3** d   **4** b   **5** g   **6** h   **7** e   **8** a   **9** c

How to…

4 1 The Italians love eating ice-cream.   **2** Children tend to watch too much television.   **3** Students usually have to get jobs in their holidays.   **4** The rich are getting richer every day.   **5** People in Australia generally spend a lot of time outside.   **6** The British eat a lot of roast beef.   **7** Japanese workers don't tend to/tend not to take a lot of holidays.   **8** Teenagers don't usually listen to jazz or classical music.

Listening

5 1 b   **2** a   **3** d   **4** c
1 Americans   **2** on time   **3** telephone   **4** usually   **5** shake hands   **6** business card   **7** offer   **8** money

Reading

6 1 B   **2** A   **3** A   **4** B   **5** A   **6** A

Lesson 11.3
Grammar

1 1 had walked   **2** had died   **3** had never met   **4** didn't find   **5** had sent   **6** spent   **7** ate   **8** told   **9** hadn't walked   **10** had invented

2 1 slept / hadn't slept   **2** took / hadn't taken   **3** saw / hadn't seen   **4** ate / hadn't eaten

3 1 I'd / had promised to visit a friend   **2** We'd / had gone to bed.   **3** I'd / had my breakfast already.   **4** I hadn't booked a room.   **5** I'd / had forgotten my credit card.

Pronunciation

4 example: stressed   **1** unstressed   **2** unstressed   **3** unstressed   **4** stressed   **5** unstressed

Writing

5a people: shy, friendly **weather:** cloudy, sunny **transport:** regular, comfortable **food:** delicious, tasty **countryside:** mountainous, green **city:** crowded, exciting

b 1 weather   **2** transport   **3** countryside

c 1 We arrived at the *crowded /exciting* market.   **2** There were *friendly* faces smiling from every corner.   **3** A *shy* girl walked past with a basket of flowers. She looked at her feet.   **4** An old lady sold her *tasty /delicious* salads, ready to eat.   **5** We drove in a *comfortable* taxi through the *crowded* city centre.   **6** The weather was good, so we enjoyed a *delicious /tasty* lunch on the *sunny* balcony, and watched the *mountainous* view.

Unit 12 Money

Lesson 12.1
Vocabulary: money nouns

1 1 lend   **2** won   **3** withdraw   **4** earn   **5** borrow   **6** sales

2 1 B   **2** C   **3** C   **4** B   **5** A   **6** A   **7** B

Grammar: second conditional

3 1 If I was friends with Madonna, I would take her to Burger King. (Miki, 10)   **2** I would visit my grandfather in California every holiday if I had my own aeroplane. (Serhat, 11)   **3** I would have dinner with Julia Roberts if I met her. (Luke, 10)   **4** If I spoke many languages, I would talk to all the people in the world. (Elle, 6)   **5** I would write emails to my friends if I had a computer. (Reuben, 10)   **6** If I sang well, I would start my own band. (Li, 10)   **7** I would buy a Mercedes if I was rich enough. (Tim, 7)   **8** If I went to Argentina, I would play football with Diego Maradona. (Elena, 10)

4 **1** If I was better at football, I would play in the first team. **2** If she wasn't so busy, she would have time to see us. **3** If she knew his number, she would call him. **4** If I didn't already have a dog, I would get a cat. **5** If he ate more, he wouldn't be hungry all the time. **6** If I lived in Brazil, I would have to speak Portuguese.

5 **1** If I had more time, **I'd learn** a new language. **2** What would you do **if you lost** your wallet? **3** If I **had** a holiday, I'd go to Mauritius. **4** We wouldn't **drive** to work if we lived nearer the office. **5** She'd be here now if it **was** possible. **6** If you left your country, **would you** miss it? **7** I would sleep all morning if I **had** the chance. **8** If I **wasn't so lazy**, I wouldn't enjoy beach holidays.

Reading

6a **1** N **2** W **3** NW **4** X **5** NW **6** W **7** X **8** N **9** W **10** X

b **1** a **2** c **3** c

Lesson 12.2
Vocabulary: education

1 **1** Brigitte **2** Juan **3** Alessandra **4** Juan **5** Brigitte

2 **1** results **2** subjects **3** retake **4** lectures **5** passed **6** teacher

Grammar: reported speech

3 **1** Lola told Mick that he could go and buy some bread. **2** Mick said that he didn't have any money. **3** Lola told Mick that that was nothing new. **4** Mick said that he would go to the bank. **5** Lola told Mick that he didn't have a bank account. **6** Mick said that he was going to open a bank account. **7** Lola told Mick that he was going to need a job first. **8** Mick said that he wasn't hungry any more.

4 **1** I'll meet John at home at 6.00. **2** My sister isn't going to Germany. **3** Your dinner is in the oven. **4** I was too busy to visit Renzo yesterday. **5** I have taken the keys. **6** I have a meeting at 10.30. **7** You can buy some milk. **8** The car is ready.

5 **1** He said that that was the best ice-cream soda he had ever tasted. **2** He said that that had been a great game of golf. **3** He said that Luisa always arrived just as he was leaving. **4** He said that that he was bored. **5** He said that it had all been most interesting. **6** He said that dying was the last thing he would do. **7** He said that last words were for stupid people who hadn't said enough.

How to ...

6 **1** I'd rather not say. **2** Sorry, what do you mean? **3** That's a good question. **4** It's difficult to say. **5** Can I think about it for a moment?

Writing

7a **1** recently **2** grateful **3** send **4** about **5** Could

b **1** I recently saw your **2** I'd like to know more about **3** could you tell me **4** I'd be grateful if you could **5** could you send me

Lesson 12.3
Vocabulary: verbs + prepositions

1 **1** to **2** for **3** at **4** with **5** for **6** for **7** on **8** for **9** with

2 **1** (1) Hi Jim, I just had a terrible week. First I argued **(2)** with my parents because I was playing **(3)** with the dog and she broke an expensive vase. I apologised **(4)** for breaking it, but my parents said I had to pay **(5)** for the vase. I didn't have any money, so I applied **(6)** for a job in a restaurant in town. I had to wait **(7)** for ages before my interview. I was listening **(8)** to music on my Walkman and I fell asleep. When I woke **(9)** up, the boss was looking **(10)** at me. It was the worst week I've had for a long time.

Grammar: both / neither / either

3 **1** T **2** F **3** F **4** T **5** F **6** F **7** T **8** F

4 **1** Both **2** Neither **3** both **4** Neither **5** either **6** both **7** Both **8** either

Listening

5a Do exercises on the internet 5 Read Spanish books and newspapers 4 Listen to cassettes 6 Write emails to a Spanish friend 1 Do a conversation exchange 3 Travel to a Spanish-speaking country 2

b **1** F **2** T **3** T **4** F **5** F **6** T

6a **1** b **2** a **3** b **4** b **5** a **6** b

Review and consolidation units 10-12
The definite article (*the*) and phrasal verb

1 **1** When I was in Mexico I picked **up** a little Spanish. **2** This is **the** man who I told you about. **3** When she was a child she looked up **to** her father. **4** John Brown grew **up** in a big, happy family. **5** Golf is **the** best sport in the world. **6** I was brought **up** on a farm when I was a child, so I've always loved animals. **7** There are two cinemas here; **the** cinema on Brand Street is very small. **8** I've found a great restaurant; I came across **it** when I went for a walk yesterday. **9** Jack was **the** most intelligent student I've ever taught. **10** I have to **look** after my little sister because she's feeling sick.

Countable/uncountable nouns

2 **1** many **2** many **3** a little **4** much **5** any **6** much **7** many **8** many **9** a few **10** a little

Present Perfect with just/yet/already

3 **1** yet **2** already **3** already **4** just **5** already **6** just **7** already **8** yet **9** just **10** already

Present Perfect

4 **1** hadn't been **2** had gone **3** went **4** had left **5** hadn't worked **6** worked **7** hadn't seen **8** had started **9** Had he found **10** drove

Second conditional

5 **1** had / would buy **2** would stay / could **3** didn't work / would you like **4** would / weren't **5** Would you do / paid **6** were / would **7** wouldn't sleep / drank **8** stopped / would save **9** She would call / had **10** had / wouldn't live

Reported speech

6
1 They told me that they both liked fish. **2** I said that neither of my brothers had been to university. **3** She told me that she couldn't dance. **4** He said that it would rain later. **5** He told me that he had lost his watch. **6** They said that they didn't have any money. **7** She told me that she wouldn't tell anyone my secret. **8** He said that he would either go to China or India for his holiday. **9** She told me that both of her dogs slept all day. **10** I said that neither of my sisters had travelled much.

Vocabulary

7 **1** shake **2** appeals **3** miss **4** apply **5** passed **6** spend **7** depends **8** retake **9** book **10** worry

b **1** mouse **2** pension **3** tip **4** lecture **5** race **6** subject **7** deal **8** transport **9** salary **10** cash